"*Evangelism for the Rest of Us* by Mike Bechtle shows how each of us, whatever our personality style, can share our faith in a joy-giving, joy-receiving way. A splendid book."

Ken Blanchard, coauthor, *The One-Minute Manager®* and *The Secret*

"Many Christians have chosen to sit in the 'evangelism dugout' because they don't feel qualified to be on the field. But they've been playing the wrong position. Mike Bechtle's exploration of evangelism helps people discover the unique position God designed them to play and gives them hope and encouragement to get back in the game."

Dave Dravecky, best-selling author and founder of Outreach of Hope

"If you struggle with sharing your faith, like I do, then Mike's book will be significant. His personal stories and practical ideas are wrapped in a biblical perspective with lots of engaging humor. This book will take a heavy burden of guilt off your shoulders and replace it with the joyful confidence of, 'OK! I can—and want—to share Jesus!'"

Kathy Collard Miller, speaker and author of *Partly Cloudy with Scattered Worries*

"The evangelism fear factor fades when we simply 'love people and talk to them.' Whether you are an introvert or extrovert, sharing Christ is all about making room for natural relationships with the people in your everyday world. In his book, Mike

Bechtle winsomely coaches us all toward authentically living this truth in a most user-friendly way."

Fred Wevodau, National Director of
Urban Ministries for the Navigators

"Mike's book touched a chord in my heart as I saw him gently but relentlessly peel away the layers of excuses most of us hide behind. For too many years I practiced the most common and comfortable form of evangelism: I didn't! Now I'm working on Mike's three keys to overcoming fear: stay close to God for integrity of character, stay close to unbelievers for opportunities to influence, and stay close to believers for accountability and partnership. Mike's book didn't make me feel guilty for my failure to share—he is far too kind to engage in that type of negative motivation. Instead, he has written a warm and practical book on evangelism that gives me hope. God wants to partner with me in impacting people's lives eternally, and he wants me to be myself when I do so. Thanks, Dr. Mike. Because of your book, I'm more purposeful about my evangelistic efforts and more confident that God will use me the way I am to lead people to himself."

Dr. Andrew W. Neillie, president,
the Deep in the Heart Leadership Group

evangelism
for the
rest of us

SHARING CHRIST
WITHIN YOUR PERSONALITY STYLE

Mike Bechtle

BakerBooks
Grand Rapids, Michigan

© 2006 by Mike Bechtle

Published by Baker Books
a division of Baker Publishing Group
P.O. Box 6287, Grand Rapids, MI 49516-6287
www.bakerbooks.com

Printed in the United States of America

Library of Congress Cataloging-in-Publication Data
Bechtle, Mike, 1952–
    Evangelism for the rest of us : sharing Christ within your personality style / Mike Bechtle.
        p.   cm.
    Includes bibliographical references (p.   ).
    ISBN 10: 0-8010-6590-9 (pbk.)
    ISBN 978-0-8010-6590-3 (pbk.)
    1. Evangelistic work. 2. Typology (Psychology)—Religious aspects—Christianity. 3. Introversion. I. Title.
    BV3793.B38 2006
    269.′2—dc22   2005033205

Published in association with the literary agency of Alive Communications, Inc., 7680 Goddard Street, Suite 200, Colorado Springs, Colorado 80920.

For my wife, Diane,
who believes in me just the way I am
and lets me believe in her the way she is . . .

. . . a long, loving partnership
with my very best friend

contents

acknowledgments

Authors get one page to explain how their book actually made it into print. Inevitably, it's not because they were wizards of words. It's because other people participated in the process. Without them, most ideas would still be in the author's head. It takes other people to tell you that you have something to say and that you have the ability to put it in writing, and to get off your behind and start putting it on paper.

That could make for a long list, since our thoughts are shaped by every encounter we have in our lifetime. So I hereby acknowledge everyone who has been part of that process. You know who you are, and I'm more than grateful.

Specific to this book, however, are a few special individuals who were more than instrumental in making it happen:

Jim Wright initially gave me the opportunity to present these ideas for Sonlight Fellowship, an adult class at the First Evangelical Free Church of Fullerton, California. I'm grateful to the members of that class for challenging my thinking as these ideas took shape. In one session, Dr. Janice Strength said four words that freed me to put words on paper: "That's why intro-verts write."

Dan Prince, Glenn Meadows, and Jeremy Dorse have been my champions over coffee to keep me motivated. Gentlemen, know you're appreciated.

My wife and I have the privilege of serving as mentors in Becoming One, a class of young married couples at the First Evangelical Free Church of Fullerton. A big chunk of our hearts reside with them, and they keep us young. They have been sounding boards for the content as well. Special thanks to Robert Bleker and Greg Bock for the lunch meetings to discuss these ideas.

Kathy Collard Miller told me I could write. Then she gave me encouragement and advice on how she does it. She and her husband, Larry, have always been there for friendship and support. Thanks, guys, for being in our lives.

I'm hard on agents. Andrea Christian started the process, then went to work for a publisher. Then Chip MacGregor took my manuscript through labor and delivery and promptly left the profession. Now Beth Jusino is shepherding my words. Hopefully, I won't cause the same result with her. All three have been agents with Alive Communications, which has far exceeded my expectations for an agency.

Vicki Crumpton of Baker Publishing Group spins her edito-rial magic around my words to make them coherent. I've been amazed at how good I sound when she gets hold of my ideas. If this is what it's like to work with an editor, I think I'll keep writing for a long, long time. Thanks, partner!

My son, Tim, single-handedly convinced me that I could find the time to write and showed me how to make it happen. Without his wisdom, there would be no book. My gratefulness is exceeded only by my love for you, son.

My daughter, Sara, has shaped my thinking through our many conversations over the years. She'll challenge my ideas because she cares. Starbucks was made for our times together, and I enjoy nothing more than simply being with you. Thanks for bringing Brian into our family—he's a gift. Together you gave us a granddaughter, Averie. I love you all.

Finally—Diane has given me more than twenty-eight years of love and friendship. You've always had my heart, and you always will.

1

why is it so hard?

Watching One Person's Painful Journey
through Ineffective Evangelism

I gave up on evangelism.

I don't remember exactly when, but it was a long, long time ago. I can't put my finger on the exact date, but somewhere along the line, my passion for souls took a detour.

It wasn't always that way. I actually remember a time when I looked for opportunities to witness. "You're a Christian," people said. "You'll automatically want to lead people to Christ." I knew evangelism was important. I knew the value of it. I even took classes, looked for chances to share, and prayed for opportunities.

Occasionally, I found a stranger to share with. Those were the best opportunities—the ones that felt like "real" evangelism. I would start the conversation, move quickly into presenting the gospel, and end as quickly as I had started. The person usually didn't make a commitment to Christ, but I had done my part.

For the weeks and months that followed, I would bask in the afterglow of my encounter for Christ. The pressure was off; I had witnessed. I had fulfilled my Christian responsibility, and God was pleased. Of course, I also didn't feel much of a need to share again for a while. Like a smoker after a cigarette, the encounter had temporarily satisfied. But over time the need to share began to grow.

The pattern repeated itself year after year. Share with someone, feel satisfied, let time pass, feel the need to share again.

I heard at least a hundred sermons on the Great Commission and our responsibility to carry it out. I even considered foreign missions at one point after hearing missionaries share stories about people coming to Christ like overripe fruit falling from a tree.

I knew the verses about the fields being "white unto harvest" and heard guest speakers telling us to pray for laborers—then to be willing to go ourselves. I also had heard the passages about what would happen if I didn't share with someone: their blood would be on my head, meaning I would be responsible for those who died in their sins if I didn't share with them. I wasn't sure what that meant; I just knew I would be in trouble.

I attended a small evangelical Bible college. Once each semester, classes were canceled and we attended a mandatory "day of visitation." We were each paired with a partner and then assigned to an evangelistic team for the morning—the mall team, the door-to-door team, the skid row team, and so forth. I dreaded those days and even managed to find myself ill a few times—too sick to participate. On the days I did participate, I tried to get on the skid row team. Somehow, sharing my faith felt less threatening when I could do it with a homeless person who was obviously needy. After a couple of hours, we returned to campus and shared stories about what had happened. Occasionally, someone actually reported praying with someone to receive Christ. I wondered why those stories never happened to me.

One year in the '70s, our church took part in the "I Found It" campaign. It was a nationwide effort to reach every household in America with the gospel. The premise was simple. Christians around the country put bumper stickers on their cars that read "I Found It" with no explanation—presumably to attract interest from nonbelievers. Similar billboards followed. Then, during a two-week period, a coordinated telephone effort took place in churches around the country. Each church secured phone directories that listed people by address. A church was responsible for several blocks in their neighborhood. A phone bank was established in each church, and members assembled to make scripted calls. It was a high-tech (at the time) effort to do door-to-door evangelism without knocking. Every home in the nation received a call within a two-week period, surveying residents about their spiritual interests and trying to get an opportunity to share the gospel.

I felt like it was a noble effort—but I hated it, personally. I remember sitting at the phone, working my way around the block I had been assigned, feeling like a sanctified telemarketer. I was relieved when each person told me he or she wasn't interested. I knew the campaign must be doing some good and some people around the country would come to faith through the effort. Philippians 1:18 says, "But what does it matter? The important thing is that in every way, whether from false motives or true, Christ is preached. And because of this I rejoice." I knew God was going to use the effort—but I wasn't so sure he was going to use me. I followed the script, asking people questions about their lives, but inside I felt like asking, "I'm really bothering you, aren't I? You really find this irritating and intrusive, don't you? You probably feel worse about Christianity now than you did before I called, right?" Because that's how I would feel if someone called me.

The nagging questions continued: If God wanted me to evangelize, why was it so hard? Why was it so foreign to my introvert personality? I felt like it wasn't fair. God made some people noisier than others, and it seemed easy for them. But I wasn't noisy, and I felt inferior, even displeasing to God.

One night in high school, some friends and I attended an evangelism training seminar. On Friday night, we learned the basics of sharing our faith, practicing on each other during the session. Our assignment was to share our testimony with someone before we came back the next day.

Two of us left the meeting praying for an opportunity to share with someone that night. We cruised Central Avenue in Phoenix, looking for a likely candidate. We found him at Mc-Donalds—a young employee on his break. He was sitting on one of the outdoor tables, smoking a cigarette. (Since he was smoking, we figured he was probably an unbeliever.)

We parked the car, approached him from behind, and sat on either side of him. After asking the appropriate questions, it was time to move into our presentation. I remember rushing to begin so my friend wouldn't do it first, leaving me with the necessity of finding still another person. I didn't stop until I was done. Finally I asked if he would like to pray to receive Christ. He responded, "Well, I gotta get back to work. Thanks for preaching."

I felt great. I had witnessed. I could tell people I had witnessed. If someone asked me, "When was the last time you talked to someone about Christ?" I had an answer. In fact, I could use that answer for months now. I could even drop it into casual conversations with friends: "Well, last week when I was witnessing to a guy at McDonalds . . ."

But something didn't make sense. I knew God wanted me to witness—but I always dreaded it. I knew God was supposed to give us power and boldness if we asked for it, but it never seemed to help.

Then one day I discovered that I wasn't sharing my faith. In fact, I wasn't even thinking about sharing it. I could go for weeks without feeling the need to share.

So what happened? Where did I lose my passion?

I think maybe it was never there.

I realized that my motivation for sharing was centered on guilt. Whenever I actually shared my faith, it was so God would be happy, so others would see that I was a good Christian, so I would do what I was supposed to do as an obedient child of God.

But I really didn't care about the people I was witnessing to. I just didn't want to feel guilty. I eventually quit witnessing because, subconsciously, it was easier than dealing with the constant guilt.

But guilt-based methods were what I had been taught. There were different kinds of evangelism, and some were regarded more highly than others. Though it was important to live a holy life in front of our neighbors, it didn't count as much as talking out loud to them about Christ. If we went door-to-door to share with strangers—now, that was *real* evangelism. The harder it seemed, the better it was viewed.

Occasionally, someone would try to witness to me. I'd be sitting at the mall when two people would approach—and I would cringe. As an introvert, I didn't relish the idea of an impending conversation with complete strangers. Plus, I could tell by the way they approached what their agenda was. I usually told them I was a Christian and then watched their looks of relief that they hadn't encountered a hostile subject. I tried to end the conversation as quickly as possible but was often embarrassed by their public display of excitement. Once, after discovering I was a "brother," two young men grabbed my hands and prayed loudly, thanking God for our time together. I kept my eyes closed, but I could feel the stares of the crowd passing by.

The two young men praised God for the fellowship. I prayed that I would never cause someone that kind of embarrassment. I silently wondered if God was embarrassed too.

It's hard to argue with success. Those evangelistic efforts I took part in did result in a few decisions for Christ. The percentage seemed pretty low, but it was worth the effort. After all, our pastor said, "If one person comes to Christ, the effort was worthwhile."

But it reminded me of a research project carried out by a college classmate. He decided to walk down Central Avenue in Phoenix at lunchtime and ask women to kiss him. He wanted to find out how many he would have to ask before someone took him up on it. After being repeatedly cursed and ignored, and slapped a couple of times, the ninety-eighth woman gave him a kiss.

I'm not sure what thesis he was trying to prove, but if he were to follow the Christian logic about evangelism, he would have said, "It was worth the effort, because I actually got one person to kiss me." I wondered about the other ninety-seven women, who might be more hardened than ever, more suspicious, and more wary of men approaching them on the street.

Yes, the popular methods of witnessing produced some results, but I knew how I felt when people used those methods with me. I wondered how many other people put up thicker emotional walls against Christians because of the evangelistic encounters they'd endured.

I felt guilty for even thinking that way, but I knew something wasn't right. I had been told what God expected my whole life, but it seemed so foreign to my personality. I believed God had created me with a unique design, but it seemed so incompatible with what he expected of me.

If God wanted me to witness in a certain way, why wouldn't he have given me what I needed to do it?

My conclusion: I was disobedient and just needed to try harder. Or rely on his strength more. Or pray more. Or something. Whatever it was, I wasn't doing it and really didn't know how.

Then one day a tiny seed of an idea planted itself in my mind and never left. It lay dormant for a while, though I always knew it was there. Over time it took root and began to grow.

The seed was a simple thought: *What if the problem isn't obedience? What if the things I've always been taught about evangelism aren't the full picture? What if there's more to it than what I've been told? What if God has a variety of ways we can share our faith—ways that are different from the traditional methods we've been taught?*

And that's where the journey began.

Whether you're an introvert or extrovert or somewhere in between, I invite you to join me on this journey. If the usual approaches to evangelism make you break out into a cold sweat or make you feel guilty, we'll explore these questions:

- Why is witnessing so hard for me?
- Am I at a disadvantage because of my personality type?
- Are extroverts better evangelists?
- Is what I've been told about evangelism accurate?
- How do I carry out the Great Commission?
- How do I discover my "wiring"?
- Is it OK to be afraid?
- Am I feeling guilty about evangelism when I shouldn't?
- What exactly is evangelism?

You know which approaches you respond to and which ones you don't. But the same approaches that work for you won't work for everyone, because we're all unique. In our society, more people lean toward the extrovert side than the introvert side. Since extroverts are more vocal, they're the ones who have developed most of the approaches to evangelism. For people who aren't quite that outgoing, those methods can be pretty intimidating. Either way, our purpose is the same—to bring people to Christ.

This book won't discredit any method currently in use. The purpose is to provide a new way of thinking that could put people who don't witness back on the front lines. They'll just be using methods that are uniquely suited to their personality style as they encounter the people God brings into their path.

2

looking for a simpler solution

Feeling the Need for a Unique Approach

My wife, Diane, grew up by the ocean. While we were dating, she told me about the dreaded family trips they took each summer to Arizona to visit her grandfather. They navigated the hot desert in an old Chevrolet Corvair—without air conditioning.

She also told me of her "vow" to God. She promised him she would do whatever he asked her to do—except marry a minister or live in the desert.

Two years later, we were married. I was minister of worship at our church at the time. A year later, we moved to Phoenix.

We made the drive in the middle of August, arriving when the midafternoon temperature was 117 degrees. We were convinced that God had prompted the move, but that knowledge didn't make it any easier—or cooler.

While we drove, Diane pondered her mixed feelings about the adventure. She saw the dirt, the sagebrush, the rocks, and the tall saguaro cacti with their arms pointing toward the sky. Thinking of the contrast with her beloved ocean, she said, "OK, tell me just one good thing about this desert."

I replied, "Check out the cacti—they're all lifting their hands and praising God."

Long pause. "OK, that's one. Give me another," she said.

That one example was really enough. We could find many more if we looked around. God loves the coastline just as much as we do, but he also loves the desert. And the mountains, and the prairies, and the oceans white with foam . . .

No matter what the terrain, everything in creation does what God designed it to do. Cacti grow up, not down. Wind blows. Rocks lie there. Snakes slither. Birds fly. Flowers bloom on schedule.

There's really only one part of creation that regularly tries to operate outside God's design. That's us. For some reason, we often try to be something we're not. If we actually figure out how we're supposed to live, we assume everybody else should live that way too. So we tell everyone else how they should function. After all, it works for us—shouldn't it work for other people as well?

One of a Kind

Ephesians 2:10 says God made us with a unique design. It says we are his "workmanship." The Greek word *poema* is used in this passage, which is where we get the word *poem*. When God wanted to express his creativity, he didn't write a poem or paint a picture. He made us. We're the ultimate expression of his creativity. It would only make sense that if he designed us with a unique purpose, he would want us to function in that way.

Imagine going to the doctor because you have a sore throat. After a few minutes, the doctor opens the door to the examination room, peeks inside, and says, "How can I help you?" You describe your symptoms.

"OK, I'm going to prescribe a cast for your arm," he says.

"But my arm's OK—it's my throat that hurts," you protest.

"Yes," he replies, "but I'm still going to prescribe a cast. It's a good solution. I've prescribed hundreds of casts, and they've all worked extremely well. In fact, I've become kind of an expert on casts. I've had special training from the top cast makers in the country. Trust me—it's the best thing for you."

I'm guessing your confidence level in that doctor would be pretty low. For one thing, he prescribed without examining you. For another, he was more interested in his solution than in your situation. You'd probably escape as quickly as possible and never return. You'd tell your friends about the experience to ensure that they would avoid that doctor as well.

Most people have discovered that life is easier when we use things the way they're designed to be used. If we want to cut down a tree, we use a chain saw, not a razor blade. Yes, it would be possible to do it with a razor blade, but that's not what a razor blade is best at. It would take much more time and effort. On the other hand, you wouldn't cut an article out of the newspaper with a chain saw—a razor blade would do a much better job.

God designed us with a specific purpose in mind. The reason? So we could do what he wants us to do, in the unique way that nobody else could do it. Why should we try to do it differently?

If God designed introverts, doesn't it make sense that he would want them to do his work through that personality? When introverts spend time trying to function like extroverts, they're doing more than just wasting time. They're actually robbing themselves of the very tools God gave them to do his work.

In the same way, it wouldn't make sense for extroverts to function like introverts. God made extroverts to do extrovert things. He made introverts to do introvert things. Both are essential for society to function, and both are necessary for the church to accomplish God's purposes. Paul said, "If the whole body were an eye, where would the sense of hearing be? If the whole body were an ear, where would the sense of smell be? But in fact God has arranged the parts in the body, every one of them, just as he wanted them to be" (1 Cor. 12:17–18).

I Gotta Be Me

Tom worked for twenty-three years as a high-tech engineer in the defense industry, developing the fine circuitry that guided missiles to their destination and caused bombs to explode properly. When I met him, he was working as an engineer in a company that designed pacemakers for heart patients. His job was designing the intricate systems that keep a person's heart beating in a regular rhythm. Curious, I asked him why he had transitioned to such a radically different career. "Oh, I'm doing the same thing I've always done," he said. "The type of circuitry I design is almost identical. But I spent twenty-three years designing things that would kill people. I decided it was time to start keeping them alive instead."

Tom was good at what he did and was able to employ his skills and passion in his work. He used the best of how he was wired but chose different paths for carrying out that passion. When he changed companies, he didn't start from scratch, doing something he wasn't designed to do. He just took his skill set to another field of work.

Everyone has parts of their job they love to do and parts they could do without. You probably find that the daily responsibilities you enjoy the most are the things you're wired to do. The things you dread are probably the farthest from the way you're designed.

That's the problem with people who take a job that is uncomfortable but pays well. They probably won't excel in that position, because it's not who they are. But other people might take a lower paying job they love and flourish because it's simply an extension of who they are by design.

Yesterday I spoke with Jorg, a captain of a cruise ship. He said, "I've never had a job. I just get up every morning and do what I love to do best. They pay me to do it, so I've never had to work."

That's true in our Christian lives as well. We'll find our greatest fulfillment and joy in doing the things God designed us to do and the greatest frustration when we work outside our unique, God-given design. That's why so many introverts are frustrated with evangelism: we've been told how it needs to happen, but that's not how we're wired. It's not that we don't want to share; it's just too foreign to our temperament.

Common Sense

I've spent a great portion of my life trying to be something I'm not. What started out as a genuine concern for the lost gradually changed to a guilt-based approach to winning them to Christ. After years of doing something that took so much work and produced so much stress with so few results, I gave up. If there had been some fruit, it might have been different. It was even worse when I heard sermons that said I should be faithful even if there weren't any results. It just didn't make sense. I wasn't convinced that I was being faithful to the right things. I began to suspect that I was being faithful to someone else's idea of what evangelism should look like, not God's customized idea of evangelism for me.

After discussing these ideas over the past few years, I've found several common themes in people's responses:

1. "I really want to evangelize."

Deep down inside, most sincere believers want to evangelize—not just because it's expected but because they have a genuine desire to help others find the answer to life's issues. But when people who are not naturally outgoing are told what evangelism is supposed to look like, it's more than scary. It's like going on a Christian version of *Fear Factor*. They'd rather eat live bugs or bungee jump from a burning hot-air balloon than share their faith in the ways they've been taught.

2. "It would be easier if I were more outgoing."

Western culture seems to value extroversion. If a person wants to get ahead in life, in business, or in relationships, being an extrovert seems to be an advantage. Surrounded by that paradigm, it's easy for an introvert to feel cheated. But that attitude overlooks the doors that can be opened only by quiet persuasion.

3. "I've tried, but I don't see any results."

The desire to share the Good News with others seems to be hardwired into most Christians. New believers want to tell others but don't know how. So they listen to tapes, read books, and hear sermons on witnessing techniques. For introverts, those methods seem pretty unnatural, but since they have the desire, they try them anyway—with little result. That leads to discouragement and guilt. It's not that the methods they've learned are bad; it might be simply that they need a more complete list of methods.

4. "I don't know how to lead someone to Christ."

My daughter, Sara, and her husband, Brian, are in a Bible study for young married couples. Recently the group members were discussing their various perspectives on evangelism. They all had a desire to share their faith, but not one person in the group knew how to lead someone to Christ. It simply had not been part of their upbringing. When I was at their stage of life, I knew how to share but didn't want to in the way I had been taught. They wanted to share but didn't know how.

5. *"There has to be a better way."*

Could there be more to the process of evangelism than we've been told? We know God wouldn't give us the desire to share our faith without giving us the tools to do it. Like David trying to fight in Saul's armor, we find the tools we've been given unnatural. We're on a quest to find new tools.

Chuck Swindoll is known internationally for his giftedness in the pulpit. His ability to communicate has been a tool to lead many people closer to the kingdom. When he pastored the church I attended, we took every opportunity to sit under his teaching. It was a chance to see someone truly using the gifts he had been given.

Sometimes our minister of music would have Chuck join him in an impromptu duet during the service. Chuck would always jump at the chance. He had a great voice and loved to sing, but his gifts were in preaching, not singing. People came to hear him preach and would have been mightily disappointed if he had given a concert instead of a sermon. Just visit any Christian bookstore; you'll find a whole shelf of his books, but you'll be hard-pressed to find a CD of his music.

I've gone to a few Christian concerts where the artists talked for about ten minutes between songs. Usually it was some kind of challenge about the meaning of the song we were about to hear. But I was always disappointed. They were spending too much time doing what they were not gifted to do, which robbed us of the chance to be ministered to by what they *were* gifted to do. The concerts that have meant the most to me were usually packed with music, occasionally interrupted by personal insights from the musician.

Singers are supposed to sing. Preachers are supposed to preach.

The pattern of all creation is that things do what they were designed to do. When that happens, things go smoothly. When it doesn't, there's confusion, frustration, and chaos. If we truly believe that God designed us individually and uniquely, that he shaped our future before we were born, and that he has a customized purpose for us, it follows that he has given us what we need to fulfill that design.

Being Yourself

Kevin Ryan is one of the premier guitar builders in America. He is known for the quality of his instruments and the attention he gives to detail that others might overlook. Coming from an engineering background, he would seem an unlikely person to produce musical instruments, but using his engineering skills, he approaches his craft in a way that others don't. "God is in the details," he says. Kevin doesn't give concerts, and he's not a world-class musician. He just builds world-class guitars that are sought out by world-class players.

I worked my way through college tuning pianos. I didn't know how to play; I just tuned them. I always had a good ear and could make an instrument sound great, but after I tuned people's pianos, they usually expected a mini concert. "Play something," they'd say. They were almost always surprised that I didn't know how to play, but as soon as they sat down to try out the instrument, they noticed how much their playing had improved (or at least, it sounded like it). They didn't care that I didn't play, because my tuning skills gave them what they needed to play better.

In both cases, the musician is the person people notice. But that performer's success is dependent on the people who build and maintain the instruments. No one expects a great concert from the support staff any more than they expect the musician to be an expert in building instruments. Each person does what he or she is uniquely gifted to do. God wants each of us to share our faith, but he wired us uniquely so we could share uniquely. Our effectiveness comes through our uniqueness. The more we work through our God-given temperament, the more effective we'll be in ministering to others.

I love hearing J. P. Moreland speak. An author, philosopher, and apologist, he debates unbelievers in universities and auditoriums around the globe. He's a master at crafting a position while treating the other person with the utmost respect. His ability to dismantle a person's argument while affirming the person shows the artistic combination of courage and grace.

When he makes a point, my first thought is usually, *That's a great answer—I never would have thought of that.* But that doesn't bother me anymore. I've learned that I'm not wired to be a debater. I might think of great answers, but not until the next day. That could make for a really long debate. I'm really glad to be on the same team as J. P. Moreland, but I don't have to *be* J. P. Moreland. I don't have to hold big crusades like Billy Graham or Greg Laurie either.

I've gotta be me.

God designed us the way he did so we could carry out his purposes in a unique way. Nobody else can be me as well as I can. If we compare ourselves with others or strive to be like them, we rob people of the very things God wants to give them through us.

Our particular personality type isn't something to be cured— it's something to be celebrated!

3

innies and outies

Exploring Different Personality Types, from Introvert to Extrovert

In a sporting goods store a few years ago, I tried on several different pairs of ski goggles. Each had a different color lens. The clerk suggested that amber-colored lenses gave the best visibility in poor weather conditions such as fog or haze. When I put the goggles on, the entire store became brighter and sharper. The problem was that everything was yellow.

I tried on other pairs of goggles and found that the color of the lens impacted my view of everything I looked at. Red goggles made everything red; blue goggles made everything blue.

My son was with me, trying on other goggles. He put on blue lenses, while I put on red. Then we picked a jacket across the room and tried to determine what color it was. I was convinced the jacket was red; he was convinced it was blue. We could have debated all day, but we wouldn't have changed each other's minds. Our lenses determined how we saw things.

When John Gray wrote *Men Are from Mars, Women Are from Venus,* he brought out the idea that men and women are different. People realized, some of them for the first time, that not everyone views the world the same way. Since I think a certain way, I assume it's correct (it's my paradigm—how I view the world). Since I feel that way, I assume everybody else does too. So if you feel differently, I assume there's something wrong with you.

Introverts and extroverts see the world through different lenses too. We each believe that what we see through our lens is reality. That usually means that extroverts view introverts through an outgoing lens, assuming that life would be better for introverts if they could learn to be more outgoing. Introverts often feel that extroverts would function better if they could slow down and think more deeply.

Since introverts hear that message so often in society, they tend to believe it. They try to look at the world through a lens they don't have. They're looking through a red lens, trying to convince themselves that what they see is blue. The result? They feel that introversion is something that is inferior, is wrong, and needs to be corrected. So they spend the rest of their lives trying to act like extroverts but finding only frustration. They wonder why being more outgoing seems so uncomfortable and why it never seems to get any easier. Over time, their self-esteem gets lower and lower, since they're not able to cure the "problem."

Recently I was sitting in a restaurant with an extrovert. We noticed a person sitting alone in a booth across the room. I was thinking about how enjoyable it is to sit alone in a restaurant on a business trip, relaxing and savoring the meal.

Suddenly my friend said, "That poor guy."

Taken aback, I said, "What are you talking about?"

He said, "That guy over there is all alone. I feel so sorry for him. If I wasn't having dinner with you, I'd probably go over there and keep him company."

If someone did that to me while I was dining alone, it would ruin a great evening. My friend was viewing the person through an extrovert lens. I was viewing him through an introvert lens.

So which of us was correct?

In an adult fellowship class at our church, I was teaching about the difference between extroverts and introverts. I was pointing out the strengths that are unique to introverts—how they tend to be deep thinkers, are reflective, are good planners, and so on. An extrovert in the class interrupted and said, "Hey—I don't think I like this. It sounds like you're saying extroverts are shallow and brassy." At first I wasn't sure how to respond. But I realized she was peeking at herself, possibly for the first time, through an introvert lens. I pointed out that it was the reverse of what introverts face all the time—extroverts thinking introverts are shy, aloof loners.

The class was receptive to these concepts and was friendly to the discussion about the place of quiet personalities in evangelism, but the extroverts were the ones participating in the discussion. They agreed with the basic concepts but then began adding their own perspectives to "complete" the teaching:

- "Well, you have to talk sometime."
- "You're more of an extrovert than you think." (Referring to my platform skills)
- "God is passionate about us sharing our faith out loud."

I expected those comments, because most extroverts have not tried to see through the eyes of an introvert. What was most interesting, though, was the reaction of the introverts in the class. Without a word, you could see their reactions to the extroverts' comments. Several glanced knowingly at each other as if to say, "Here we go again" or "They just don't get it, do they?" Some simply withdrew from the discussion rather than fuel the flame (they could share their opinions with one or two others over lunch). Several simply shook their heads.

Living in an Extrovert World

In our world today, extroverts are the majority. Not only that, but the nature of their temperament often puts them in positions of influence. So we're basically living in an extrovert-flavored society. Since the nature of extroverts is verbal, we hear from them more. It's easy for introverts to feel out of place, since we hear so much from outgoing people and so little from quiet ones.

So how do people of varying temperaments function in an extrovert-driven society? Do introverts have to become extroverts to survive? The majority of books I've perused seem to indicate the necessity of change. Most describe techniques for introverts to be more outgoing and act more like extroverts as a way of coping. They seem to emphasize the need to *appear* to be outgoing, while they deemphasize the unique inner strength that often comes from a quiet spirit.

When Stephen Covey was conducting research for his book *The Seven Habits of Highly Effective People*, he studied 200 years of literature concerning success. The first 150 years emphasized *character*—you had to *be* the right person on the inside. But the next 50 years switched to an emphasis on *personality*—how you came across to others.

Back in the 1960s, I read a book whose premise sounded good on the surface. The author indicated that when we first meet someone, we form an impression within the first few minutes. That impression might be accurate or inaccurate, but it will be hard to change. If we feel positive about our first meeting, that person will have to do a lot of negative things before we admit that our original assessment was wrong. In the same way, if we initially feel negative, it will take a lot of positives to change our opinion.

That part was accurate. But the rest of the book went on to teach the reader how to fake it for the first few minutes so people would get a positive first impression.

Introverts tend to be extra-sensitive to how others respond to them, so it's easy to fall into the trap of acting like extroverts so people will like them. So how do introverts become comfortable with a quieter temperament while honing their social skills in an extrovert environment?

A Sliding Scale

I thought about calling this book *Extroverts Are from Lower Manhattan, Introverts Are from Bakersfield*, but I figured both cities would be offended. The sentiment, though, is the same as John Gray described in *Men Are from Mars, Women Are from Venus*. As hard as men and women try, they'll never really, experientially understand each other. Sure, they can study the opposite sex and learn about their unique needs and temperaments and perspectives, but they can never have the deep understanding that comes from living in the other person's skin.

In *The Introvert Advantage*, Marti Laney describes the extremes of the personality as "innies" and "outies," characterizing the difference between introverts and extroverts.[1] But most of us aren't at either of those extremes; we're somewhere in between.

Frank isn't comfortable with knocking on someone's door to share his faith, but he doesn't consider himself an introvert either. Anne tends to be more reflective and quiet but becomes the life of the party in a small group of friends. Both share characteristics of innies and outies, depending on the situation.

What's Your Type?

For each question below, circle the answer that best describes you in most situations.

1. When I do something complicated, I have to break it down into small steps so I don't get overwhelmed.

   Always   Sometimes   Never

2. When I'm in a meeting, I listen to everything that's said, then go off by myself to think through my feelings and opinions.

   Always   Sometimes   Never

3. I enjoy going to a restaurant by myself.

   Always   Sometimes   Never

4. At a noisy, crowded social event, I will go into the restroom for a few minutes just to get a little space.

   Always   Sometimes   Never

5. Even if I enjoy a social gathering, I look forward to the end.

   Always   Sometimes   Never

6. I would rather have a few close friends than a lot of casual ones.

   Always   Sometimes   Never

7. I'm a good listener.

   Always   Sometimes   Never

8. I don't share my opinion until I've thought it through carefully.

   Always   Sometimes   Never

9. I'd rather communicate by email than by phone.

   Always   Sometimes   Never

10. I use up energy in a group and need time alone to recharge.

    Always   Sometimes   Never

11. I usually can sense what other people are feeling, even when others can't.

    Always   Sometimes   Never

12. I dislike returning merchandise to a store.

    Always   Sometimes   Never

13. I usually prefer an evening at home to going out with friends.

    Always   Sometimes   Never

14. I prefer a quiet restaurant to a noisy one.

    Always   Sometimes   Never

15. I'd rather see a movie on its last day in the theater (when the theater is empty) than go with the opening day crowd.

    Always   Sometimes   Never

16. People say I'm creative.

    Always   Sometimes   Never

17. If I have several days where I'm constantly interacting with people, I might crash on my first quiet day.

    Always   Sometimes   Never

18. I enjoy having people stay at my house, but only for a couple of days.

    Always   Sometimes   Never

19. I tend to think before taking action (maybe too much).

    Always   Sometimes   Never

20. I procrastinate on making decisions, because I don't want to make the wrong choice.

    Always   Sometimes   Never

Give yourself three points for each "always," two points for each "sometimes," and one point for each "never." Here's what your score says about you:

20–30—Even if you enjoy being alone at times, you tend to be more of an extrovert. You gain your energy by being around other people. If you spend too much time alone, you'll automatically start making contact with people. You tend to develop your thoughts while you're talking with others. It's harder for you to take time to be alone, but alone time is still necessary for reflection and balance.

30–45—You probably enjoy people but have a strong need to catch your breath after social gatherings. You gain energy during your quiet times, but once you've built up that energy, you have to use it somewhere—so you look for social encounters. If those encounters last too long, or if they're too draining, you sense the need to pull away again.

45–60—You're an introvert, and it's not abnormal. Contrary to what you've been told, it's not something that needs to be fixed. You have unique strengths that extroverts don't have, but you'll be able to use those strengths only if you have "fuel" to function. For you, that fuel is produced when you're alone. If your schedule gets too hectic and you don't have time to yourself, you'll run out of gas.

What does it all mean? If you leave an extrovert alone for a few hours, he or she starts getting low on energy and has to call someone, but put an introvert in a social situation for a few hours, and he or she will start getting low on energy and have to retreat for a while. Introverts don't need therapy—they need renewal. For introverts, time alone does what a good meal does for someone who is hungry: it gives them fuel. As one introvert says, "I'm OK, you're OK—in small doses."

What We Know about Personalities

Back in the early 1900s, Katharine Briggs wondered why her daughter Isabel's new husband was so different from the other members of her family. She came across Carl Jung's research regarding different types of personalities. Isabel (whose last name was Myers) became interested in her mother's study and developed a questionnaire to help people identify their unique temperaments. Today millions of people have taken the Myers-Briggs Type Indicator to understand why they're different from other people they know.

The results place people along four different continuums:

1. *Extroversion* (gaining energy from people) or *Introversion* (gaining energy by being alone)
2. *Sensing* (taking in information through the senses) or *Intuiting* (seeing patterns and possibilities)
3. *Thinking* (making logical, objective decisions) or *Feeling* (making intuitive, personal decisions)
4. *Perceiving* (recognizing a banana) or *Judging* (deciding the banana would taste good)[2]

David Keirsey devised a different way of describing these unique temperaments:

1. *Artisans* (act on impulse, want to impact people)
2. *Guardians* (want to belong, know where they fit, want facts and details)
3. *Rationals* (want knowledge and logical answers, must accomplish something)
4. *Idealists* (want meaning and understanding of life, need to be authentic, creative)[3]

This doesn't mean we're squarely pigeonholed into one particular spot on the Myers-Briggs continuums or that we're exclusively defined by one of Kiersey's categories. It means that

- we're a unique combination of temperament traits

- we all function to some degree in all of those traits
- some characteristics will apply to us more than others
- we're different from other people

I am right-handed. That doesn't mean I don't use my left hand at all; it just means that most of the time, I'll reach for something with my right hand first. In the same way, I have certain temperament traits that uniquely define me. That doesn't mean I never work outside those traits, but usually I'll use those traits first when dealing with a situation.

Extroverts: Solar Panels

When Joe has a Saturday off, he wants to hit the golf course early. He's already set up his foursome earlier in the week and confirms with each of them on his cell phone before arriving at the course. He may have been tired when he woke up, but his energy rises along with his score as he converses from hole to hole. Joe asks his fellow golfers if they want to go out to lunch when they're finished playing. Once back at home, he's able to work by himself in the garage for a few hours, because he's built up energy throughout the morning. But after a while, he wanders over to his neighbor's house to talk about his landscaping project.

Laney would describe Joe as an extrovert.[4] Like a solar panel, he gets recharged by being out in the open, drawing energy from his conversations with others. He's able to function alone but feels drained after a few hours. Joe will instinctively seek others out when that happens.

Celebrating Extroversion

Since extroverts are society's majority, they usually don't feel out of place. They're comfortable in their environment, because they're surrounded by people with similar temperaments. We're familiar with the characteristics of extroverts, because they're obvious. By their very nature, extroverts are "out in the open" where we don't have to try to discover their qualities. Here are some of the unique characteristics of extroverts:

- *They reach outward to get their energy.* Extroverts build inner strength from being around others. They find energy in a noisy, crowded room and are often disappointed when a party has to end. If their car stereo and the air conditioner break at the same time, they'll probably get the stereo fixed first so they don't have to drive in a quiet car.
- *The bigger the group, the better they function.* Not all extroverts are party animals, but they love the dynamic atmosphere of a group. When a movie opens, they want to be in line at the premier to see everything that's happening. If one person invites them out for coffee, they'll ask if they can bring two others.
- *They think out loud.* They're active participants in a group discussion and think by interacting with others. They'll toss ideas into the discussion before thinking them through just to see how others react. It's often hard for them to process ideas deeply when they're alone. They're usually considered good group members because of their participation and energy.
- *The more friends they have, the better.* Extroverts have a few close friendships but interact with as many people as possible. They enjoy learning other people's perspectives and talking with new acquaintances.
- *They prefer talking to writing.* The phone is their friend. If extroverts want to know something, they'll call and ask. Email is often a tedious necessity, because they have to develop their thoughts in writing without talking to someone else about it.

- *They prefer multitasking.* They can juggle many tasks at a time and are often seen as high performers. In general, they accomplish a great deal, but sometimes they have trouble completing tasks because they have so many things on their plate at once.

Introverts: Rechargeable Batteries

Deb doesn't consider herself to be shy and often enjoys the company of friends. When she attends luncheons with people she doesn't know, she's able to engage in conversation easily, but when she arrives home, she wonders why she is so tired. During the afternoon, Deb lets the answering machine pick up because she just doesn't feel like talking. The radio stays off, or she puts on a CD with relaxing music. It feels great to spend an hour or two reading or gardening. After dinner she's built up enough energy to go out for coffee with friends.

According to Laney, Deb is an introvert.[5] Like a rechargeable battery, she can produce a lot of energy for a period of time. But after a while, she needs time alone to refuel without anyone around.

Last week I got a new cell phone. The full charge I put on it lasted about six days with some pretty frequent use. Today the battery went dead, so I put it on the car charger and tried to make some calls. But I discovered that this particular phone doesn't work off the charger—it only works off the battery. The charger simply recharges the battery.

I can't make any calls until the battery is charged. That's unfortunate, because I was planning on making several important calls this morning. But no matter how urgent the calls are, I can't make them with that phone. It's a really good phone, but it's out of fuel.

I guess my cell phone is an introvert. It handled lots of conversations for a few days, but now it needs some time "alone" to recharge.

Celebrating Introversion

Jonathan Rauch, a columnist for *Atlantic Monthly*, said introverts are "among the most misunderstood and aggrieved groups in America, possibly the world."[6] What's even more interesting is that introverts aren't just misunderstood by extroverts; they're often misunderstood by themselves, since they've accepted the outgoing lens as the correct one. They haven't learned that introversion is something to be celebrated, not cured.

Most introverts would like to be more outgoing, since they live in a society that values extroversion. They've heard extroverts described as confident, strong, and normal. They've heard introverts described as shy, reserved, and slow. But why would God have made different personality types if he wanted us all to be extroverts?

Psalm 139 says God fashioned us in the womb. When we were born, we were the perfect expression of his perfect design. He made us just the way he wanted us and didn't make any mistakes. As the old adage goes, "God don't make no junk."

At least one-fourth of the population is made up of introverts. Others might not consider themselves introverts, but they're quieter than other people. So what did God have in mind when he created them? Here are some of the unique characteristics of introverts:

- *They reach inward to get their energy.* Like a rechargeable cell phone, they gain strength during their downtimes. They build up energy in a quiet environment, then go out and use it up. They might enjoy a social gathering but enjoy the end of it even more.

- *They function best in smaller social settings.* It doesn't mean they're necessarily shy. They probably like people, but not too many. They'll go to Starbucks with one or two people but get drained as the number increases.
- *They enjoy a quiet environment.* Put them in a noisy environment, and they'll get drained quickly. They often drive with the radio turned off, or if they're concentrating to find an address, they'll turn the radio down so they can think more clearly.
- *They do their best thinking alone.* When a group is problem solving, they'll listen carefully, but they need time alone after the meeting to sort through their thoughts.
- *They tend to be good listeners.* They don't blurt out answers but think through their responses before sharing them. Sometimes they're not seen as strong group members because they don't say much. But they're taking it all in, summarizing what's said, and can come back with a strong solution later. They make good eye contact when listening but tend to look away when speaking.
- *They think deeply.* They're often the ones who come up with new ideas (after the meeting). They won't often share in the group but will approach the leader after the meeting to share their thoughts.
- *They don't like shallow relationships.* They prefer having a few close friendships to interacting with multiple acquaintances. Small talk has little value to them. When they ask someone, "How are you?" they really want to know and are frustrated if the person answers, "Fine."
- *They often prefer to communicate in writing.* Since they do their best thinking after a conversation takes place, they often feel uncomfortable on the phone or in a fast-paced conversation. Sometimes they feel frustrated because they can't think on their feet like other people. But putting their thoughts in writing gives them time to process their ideas,

edit them, and deliver them in a form that communicates effectively. They often avoid talking on the phone because they can't see the person's nonverbal behavior and body language. They have no problem letting calls go to voice mail so they can listen to them and plan their responses.

- *They tend to focus on one thing at a time.* Multitasking is difficult, since they might get overwhelmed with too much stimulation. They need to focus on one thing at a time in bite-size pieces. Too many tasks can lead to procrastination, since they can't decide where to begin.

My wife, Diane, and I were at a wedding reception recently. We sat at a round table with people we knew, but the noise level was high enough in the room that conversation was difficult. As introverts, our energy was drained simply by the level of noise in the room. Having to shout to hold a conversation with tablemates made it even more exhausting.

On the other side of Diane was Joe, an introvert, who has been in our adult fellowship class for years. After a few minutes, Diane leaned over to Joe and said, "I'm guessing that since we're both introverts, and since it's really noisy in here, and since we both dislike making small talk at these kind of events, we'd both probably be really happy if we could just sit and watch people and not feel like we had to talk to each other a lot. Right?"

Joe simply responded, "Yep." I think they really enjoyed each other's company that night because they had the common bond that minimized expectations.

It doesn't matter how friendly or unfriendly we might feel; an empty tank is an empty tank. If I run out of gas on the freeway, it might be because I was too busy driving to take time to refuel. At that point, my good intentions, wishful thinking, and resolve to do it differently don't mean anything. If there's no gas, I'm not going anywhere until I refuel.

Introverts refuel by spending time alone. The purpose of refueling is to drive the car, not just to have a full tank. But without the fuel, I can't drive. In the same way, God has called us to engage others in spiritual dialogue (whether verbally, in writing, or in other creative ways), but if I don't keep an eye on the "gas gauge," my best intentions won't fill the tank. No gas, no gain.

How We're Different

Extroverts	Introverts
Reach out to get energized	Reach in to get energized
Feel drained when alone	Feel drained around people
Concentrate easily	Are distracted easily
Action-oriented	Thought-oriented
Learn by doing	Learn by watching
Same in public and private	Different in public and private
Keep emotions inside	Let emotions out
Think out loud	Think alone
Make decisions easily	Need time to make decisions
Act, think, act	Think, act, think
Verbal in large groups	Quiet in large groups

The Perfect Blend of People

God made extroverts and introverts and everything in between because society can't function without multiple personality styles.

Not every extrovert lacks the unique skills of an introvert, just as introverts vary in their personalities. Most people find themselves on a continuum between the two extremes, depending on the situation. But imagine a world with just extroverts or just introverts. A world comprised exclusively of extroverts would be noisy, driven toward accomplishment, and quick to carry out plans—but the plans could be lacking the depth that comes from introverts' quiet contemplation. In the same way, an introvert world would be peaceful and contemplative, and plans would be well thought out and defined—but the plans might never be accomplished!

The ratio of one introvert for every three extroverts matches society's need to move ahead. Progress takes more doers than thinkers, but both are necessary. Introverts are a minority in the general population, but studies have shown that they're a majority (60 percent) in the gifted population.[7] The number rises to 75 percent among the highly gifted—those having an IQ over 160.[8] Extroverts tend to dominate politics and public life, but introverts are the advisors who help shape policy behind the scenes.

Most books teach coping techniques for introverts—ways to work around social encounters or stressful situations—but that simply reinforces the problem, implying that introverts need to pretend they're extroverts. The power of introversion is tapped when we understand the following:

1. God deliberately designed introverts for a unique purpose.
2. They're not inferior, just unique.
3. They possess strengths extroverts can't live without.

Realizing God created each of us with a unique personality gives us the freedom to celebrate our unique design instead of comparing ourselves to others.

The Implications for Evangelism

For the extrovert personality, the implications for evangelism are obvious:

- Extroverts are not afraid to speak up, so they approach people easily.

- They think clearly when a conversation is taking place, so they're not intimidated by someone's questions.
- They're action oriented, so they reach a lot of people.
- They're outspoken and take risks in conversations; they're not afraid to talk about tough issues.
- They tend to get to the point quickly.

Introverts also have some unique advantages in evangelism:

- Introverts care what people think, so they'll be sensitive in their approach to others.
- They recognize their inability to reach people through an outgoing personality, so they're more aware of their dependence on God to work through them.
- As fishers of men, they see themselves as bait rather than the hook.
- Quiet people who think deeply can reach other quiet people who think deeply (the ones who are turned off by a hard-sell approach).
- They have the patience to let God use them in another person's life over a long period of time rather than focusing on an immediate decision.
- They might reach fewer people but build deeper relationships with them.

In the chapters that follow, we'll develop these ideas in a practical sense. We'll look at the common teaching on evangelism and learn why it may not go far enough.

4

which method is best?

Reshaping Current Methods
of Evangelism to Fit Our Personalities

My initial research in the area of evangelism for introverts took me to Christian bookstores. My plan was to find out what had already been written on the subject so I could learn new ways to share my faith that fit my temperament. I suspected that I wouldn't find much but would be able to look through traditional resources on evangelism and find a chapter or two devoted to introverts. I blocked out a couple of hours to visit a bookstore.

I wasn't prepared for what I found—or rather, what I didn't find.

I wandered up and down the aisles of a medium-size popular Christian bookstore in our area. The largest sections were New

Releases, Women's Issues, Family, and Devotionals. Smaller sections were devoted to Men's Issues, Christian Living, and Bible Studies. Music took up about a quarter of the floor space, and there was a similar allotment for Christian jewelry, stickers, and gifts. But nothing on evangelism.

When I finally asked for the location of the evangelism section, I was told, "We don't have one. There's not enough interest."

I spent my two hours going through the shelves title by title to see if there were any books that dealt with evangelism. I found three that turned out to be heavily slanted toward the traditional extrovert perspective. One had a chapter that acknowledged that some people tend to be "quieter" Christians, but the implication was for them to pray for boldness so God would give them courage to be "noisy" Christians.

Later visits to two other bookstores yielded similar results. Finally I went to a much larger store, which did have a section on evangelism. I found about twenty different titles, which was encouraging. The majority were extrovert focused, but several were written from a paradigm that allowed people to be who God made them.

Later, thinking about those experiences, I had two distinct thoughts:

1. According to Scripture, God has a real passion for people. He wants us to be godly people, but he also wants us to intentionally influence others toward faith.
2. The percentage of books I found that dealt with "outreach" (evangelism) was tiny compared with the percentage of books dealing with "inreach" (growth).

If people buy what they're interested in, it looks like people aren't very interested in sharing their faith.

But God is.

50

Moving from Good Sharing to Great Sharing

Evangelism isn't a new concept. From the time Christ left the future of the church in his disciples' hands, people have been sharing their faith with others. The objective has always been the same—to bring others into a relationship with Christ.

But in the past two thousand years, different perspectives have been emphasized at different times. One model suggested we present the gospel, invite people to become Christians, and welcome them into the church if they decide positively (*believing* came before *belonging*). Another model suggested we bring people into the church and let them participate in the spiritual life. That leads them to belief, and we pray with them to make a commitment (*belonging* led to *believing*).

Two different approaches, both leading to the same objective. But through the years, these types of perspectives have been hotly debated, and the controversies have taken us away from the overall purpose: bringing people to Christ. In Philippians 1:18, Paul said he really didn't care how people presented the gospel as long as they presented it.

When I was growing up, people emphasized forgiveness of sin: "If you accept Christ, your sins will be forgiven and you'll be freed from your evil past." For many people, that approach has little impact today. They've been raised in a culture of tolerance that suggests that people are basically good, even though they've made some bad choices in the past. They try to learn from their mistakes and make better choices in the future, so they don't feel a strong need to be forgiven.

Years ago I heard a message on how to share the gospel with a person who has everything. It said that people respond to something only when they feel a need. But many people have found ways to fill the inner emptiness of their lives (possessions, busyness, travel). That doesn't mean the needs no longer exist; people have just anesthetized themselves so they don't feel them. The sermon suggested that new approaches were necessary to meet people at their point of felt need.

This emphasis on different techniques of sharing is evident between personality types as well. Introverts tend to share their positions cautiously: "What about this perspective?" Extroverts tend to present their positions as fact: "This is what it means." That doesn't mean either way is right or wrong—it's just what I've observed.

Most of the books I found on evangelism were written by extroverts. When they presented their perspective, it was generally positioned as fact, as the most effective way to witness. Introverts reading those books would feel like they were doing things incorrectly if they did not follow the method presented. The authors usually reinforced their teachings with Scripture verses, but looking at the Scriptures apart from the books and in context, I found that those verses generally were much richer in truth than the authors' writings may have indicated.

The following are some of the incomplete perspectives I've found in typical resources on evangelism.

Seven Misconceptions about Evangelism

1. You haven't really witnessed to someone until you've taken that person through the plan of salvation.

I was taught that witnessing wasn't really legitimate unless you presented the entire plan of salvation, using appropriate verses to support a point-by-point description of God's plan for that person's life. But I never found that in Scripture. Even Jesus himself answered people's questions and made statements that got them thinking. But there's not a lot of evidence that he made a start-to-finish presentation of the gospel. He came close with Nicodemus (John 3), but that conversation was primarily Jesus responding to the already-interested ruler's questions. (Christ's approach is covered in more detail in chapter 8.)

The biblical model of evangelism is primarily a process, not an event. The pattern involves meeting people at their level, developing a relationship, and moving them along a notch or two in their spiritual journey. When people did make a commitment to Christ, we usually don't see a detailed presentation of the gospel. They had already gone through the steps of moving closer to Christ and now were ready to make a commitment. It wasn't a sudden event; it reflected a great deal of thought and contemplation. Even when Paul gave detailed, step-by-step explanations of God's work, he was writing to believers, not unbelievers. Paul's content was the "next level" for those believers.

2. Even when you share the gospel with someone, you're not successful until that person prays to receive Christ.

Several of the books I studied presented a sales model of evangelism. Traditional books on selling show how to develop a sense of need in potential clients, explain how your solution fits their need, and then move in for the close. Some evangelism books have picked up this pattern, emphasizing the need to press for a decision for witnessing to be considered valid.

The biblical pattern makes God responsible for the close. If someone has reached the point of making a decision, guiding him or her through the process is a natural result. But forcing a decision prematurely could produce a spiritually premature believer, which could lessen the odds of his or her long-term survival and growth.

When my daughter, Sara, was a toddler, she planted carrots in our yard. I helped her water them and care for them, but we didn't have much success. The carrots would sprout and grow, and one by one they would die. One day I found out why. Looking out the window, I saw her alone in the garden, pulling up a carrot to see if it was ready yet, then sticking it back in the ground.

The time of harvest is up to God. When he tells us it's time, then it's our privilege to lead a person to the Savior. But closing the deal isn't a requisite part of every spiritual conversation.

3. If you don't share the gospel with someone, and an hour later he or she is killed in a car accident, it's your fault that he or she will spend eternity in hell.

Ezekiel 3:18 is frequently used to motivate people to witness. The passage says, "When I [the LORD] say to an evil person, 'You will surely die,' you must warn him. If you don't speak out to warn the evil person to leave his evil way, he will die in his sin. But I will hold you responsible for his death" (NCV). I've seen that passage used in several recent popular writings about sharing your faith, but it has two inherent problems.

First, it's out of context. In the passage, Ezekiel has been directly instructed by God to speak his truth to a specific group of people. If he didn't do it, God would hold him responsible for disobedience in that specific situation. Expecting all believers to take that instruction as their own would be inappropriate. Suppose you prayed for guidance in a career decision, and God made it clear that you should move to another state and take a certain job. It wouldn't make sense for your whole church to move with you.

Peggy, a woman gifted in evangelism (and an extrovert), told me that failing to share her faith with someone would be disobedience, but it's not because of guilt-induced obligation from a verse taken out of context. It's because God has specifically called her to share her faith with the people he puts in her path. She doesn't expect that of others, because she realizes that God gave her that unique mission.

Second, this interpretation of the passage puts the responsibility for salvation on us instead of on God. If evangelism is a process, God uses many people to bring someone to faith. If one person in that chain breaks the process, God doesn't say, "Oh well—I guess we can give up on Sharon. Kathy didn't witness to her, so it's hopeless." God is drawing Sharon to himself, and he'll use other people in the process. Kathy will miss out on the privilege of sharing, and there may be an obedience issue between her and God, but her failure doesn't mean Sharon is eternally doomed.

When I was in college, we talked a lot about finding out who God wanted us to marry. We were taught that God had custom designed one person for us, and it was our job to find that person (with God's help, of course). The implication was that if we married the wrong spouse, we would spend the rest of our lives living with God's second best. We often heard, "God's second best is Satan's best."

I always struggled with the logic of that. What if the person God had designed for me blew it? What if she married *her* second best? I'd get cheated for life, and it wasn't even my fault! It didn't make sense that God's best for me could be restricted by other people's behavior.

It's God who draws us to himself and gives us eternal life. He uses other people in the process, but he's not restricted by their behavior.

4. It's important to witness to as many people as possible.

The exciting thing about our unique God-given design is that we're all so different. Not everyone can be reached by everyone. That's why he puts people in our lives we can influence. Extroverts tend to have more relationships in their lives. Introverts tend to have fewer, but deeper, relationships. Introverts will take the time to build trust in a relationship and deal patiently with someone's questions.

If we were evaluated based on the sheer number of people we shared with, we'd have trouble knowing when we were pleasing God. Do we all have to hold large crusades? What about a pastor of a five-thousand-member big-city church? Is he more spiritual than the pastor of a five-hundred-member suburban church? This kind of illogical measurement just leads to frustration. No matter how many conversations we have, there could always be one more. But it's not the quantity of the conversations we have; it's the quality of the relationships we build. Christ occasionally shared with the multitudes, but he spent more time with his twelve disciples—and was heart bonded to three of them. The result? Those three men changed the world to a greater extent than the rest of the Twelve. We don't hear much about the impact of the multitude.

Christ said, "The harvest is plentiful. . . . Ask the Lord of the harvest . . . to send out workers" (Matt. 9:37–38). Sermons often suggest that our proper response is to be the laborers—to answer the call. But the passage is clear. *In that specific instance*, Christ didn't ask them to be the laborers; he asked them to pray that God would raise up laborers.

It's God's work, not ours. He chooses us to participate at specific times in specific ways. Sometimes we're the laborers. Other times we're called to pray. We're always called to be responsive.

5. I have to be bold in my witness.

Biblical boldness isn't something we do; it's something God gives us. We're often told to pray for boldness, but then we try to *act* bolder in our own strength. That defeats the whole purpose of praying for boldness!

I pray for lots of things. Some answers come right away, but many things are just the beginning of a process. When I pray for patience, I don't receive it overnight. I can pray for a good attitude toward a grumpy associate, but I may still get upset when he's grumpy the next day. So when I pray for boldness in sharing my faith, I expect that it's the beginning of a process. I won't suddenly be bold the next day, but I'll probably encounter situations that will require a little more strength than I have on my own.

That's boldness. It's not mustering up more courage, but waiting for God to empower me. The children of Israel weren't asked to be bold enough to cross the Red Sea. They just had to get their toes in the water (which God specifically directed them to do). Then God took over and did the miracle. In witnessing, we need to be sensitive to what he's calling us to do in each situation and then watch him work.

I've discovered that *boldness* has more than one definition. Usually we think of it as being brash and outspoken, confronting people with the gospel. But boldness really means doing what God has asked us to do in each situation, relying on his strength. For me that means I can communicate things in writing that I would be hard-pressed to verbalize in a conversation.

6. *"You shall be my witnesses" is a command.*

Acts 1:8 says, "You will receive power when the Holy Spirit comes on you; and you will be my witnesses." We're told that it's not optional and that God is commanding us to go. But it's not a command; it's a description of fact. We're not told to go out and witness. We're told that we are witnesses—whether we like it or not and whether we feel qualified or not.

A witness is someone who has had firsthand experience with something. If you see a car accident, you're a witness whether you give a police report or not. Providing the report will be beneficial to the investigators and could provide a solution to a confusing dilemma. You could give a report at the accident scene, call the officers later, or write out a description of what you saw. The fact remains: you are a witness.

As Christians, we've had firsthand experience with Christ. That makes us witnesses whether we tell anyone or not. We've been called to provide the details of what we've experienced to help people through a confusing life dilemma. That could take place in a number of different forms, but the fact remains: we are witnesses. *It's not a command; it's a description.*

Matthew 28:19 states that the task is to "make disciples." Discipleship involves guiding people closer to God from whatever place they are. For unbelievers, it's moving them one step closer to salvation. For believers, it's moving them one step closer to a mature walk with God.

7. God is happy with us if we witness and upset with us if we don't.

There's something inside many of us that says God's feeling toward us is dependent on whether or not we share our faith. But to keep our theology straight, we need to separate (1) God's unconditional love for us and (2) doing his work.

When my son was little, we used to play a game about unconditional love. I'd say, "Tim, do you know how much I love you?"

He'd reply, "A whole bunch."

"Could you do anything to make me not love you?" I'd ask.

"Nope," he'd reply.

Then he'd test me. "What if I hurt Mommy? Would you still love me then?"

"Yep," I'd say. "I'd be really upset, but I would love you just as much as ever."

In his mid-twenties now, he's confident of our love, even if he doesn't always make the choices we want him to make.

God wants us to intentionally, in the way he designed us, move people closer to him. But that's not the basis for his love for us. He knows we're frail, and he works with us the way a parent works with his child. Too often we get our view of God from our relationships with our earthly fathers, which might not have been that secure.

In our church, many people have taken short-term mission trips to other countries. I did it a few years ago, and I have to admit it feels good to be involved in kingdom work. It feels even better because it involves sacrifice—time off work, vacation time, the expense of the trip, and time away from family.

Without devaluing that involvement, I've often wondered why people usually go away from home to do it. We don't usually hear someone stand up in church and say, "I feel God has called me to take a mission trip to my neighborhood. I have a neighbor who's adding a room on his house for his growing family, and he needs help. I feel that God wants me to take two weeks off work and help him with that project. I want to build a relationship with him and his family and neighbors and use that to build a bridge of love that might move him closer to faith. I'm raising support for the time I'm taking off work and would like to raise money to help provide building materials. Wanna help?"

Considering an approach like that would certainly clarify our motives.

So what *does* the Bible have to say about evangelism?

Five Things the Bible Teaches

1. Evangelism is a team effort.

The Christian life isn't an individual sport. Introverts might prefer that it were, but we need others. Scripture is full of admonitions about the teamwork of faith. The analogy of the church as a body (1 Cor. 12:12–31) describes the relationship between different types of people and how each needs the other. Some parts of the body seem less valuable than others, but they are vital for the others to function.

Years ago a pastor friend accidentally cut off his big toe with a lawn mower. After healing, he didn't expect much of an impact, but several times while standing and greeting church members after the service, he simply fell over. He was halfway to the ground before he realized he was falling. He never realized how his big toe provided the signals that kept him balanced.

If you pray with someone to receive Christ, you don't do it alone. God has already brought a string of people into that person's life to move him or her closer to faith, and then God chooses you to guide that person through that step of commitment. As Paul says, "I planted the seed, Apollos watered it, but God made it grow. So neither he who plants nor he who waters is anything, but only God, who makes things grow" (1 Cor. 3:6–7).

2. You have to hang out with non-Christians.

I taught a course in evangelism at a Christian university for about five years. One of the semester assignments was to have a twenty-minute conversation with an unbeliever sometime during the semester. Students didn't have to witness or even talk about spiritual things. They just had to have a conversation.

At the end of the first class, two students came to me in tears. They didn't know any non-Christians and didn't know where to find them. They thought the assignment was unfair and wanted to negotiate for another way of getting credit.

Over the next few days, several more students expressed similar concerns. At first I was amazed, but then I realized I wasn't that different. I knew where I could find unbelievers, but I certainly didn't have any as friends.

Christ prayed not that we would be taken out of the world but that we would be protected from Satan (John 17:15). Most Christians have separated themselves from the world for fear of being corrupted instead of praying for protection as they live among unbelievers.

Howard Hendricks, author and professor at Dallas Theological Seminary, has said that it takes most new Christians about three years to eliminate all the non-Christians from their lives. We can't influence people toward faith if we're not involved with unbelievers. Introverts might be uncomfortable pursuing a lot of relationships. For them, *quality* relationships with unbelievers is more valuable than *quantity*. But the relationships have to be formed through interaction with unbelievers. Introverts specialize in "going deep" in those life-on-life connections. That's where evangelism takes place.

3. We don't "do" evangelism—God does.

Mother Teresa said her mission in life was "to be a pen in the hand of God." God has designed each of us in a certain way, with a certain temperament, so he could use us uniquely. Evangelism is God's work; he uses us as tools to make evangelism happen (John 12:32). Our job is to lift him up before others—through the unique temperament God has gifted us with. When we do, he'll work in people's hearts.

If God is the one bringing people to himself, then we'll want to do it his way. For example, Scripture emphasizes the importance of praying for those who haven't come to faith. When we pray for people, we're recognizing that salvation is God's work, not ours.

A former colleague of mine began a ministry years ago that focused on the power of prayer in evangelism. His approach assumes that not everyone is ready for a gospel presentation but that everyone encounters situations for which they need prayer. So he approaches people, even door-to-door, asking if there is anything for which they would like prayer. If they say no, he doesn't take it any further. If they have a specific prayer request, he'll either pray for them right then, offer to pray later, or both. A few weeks later, he'll make another casual contact to remind them that he's been praying and to ask how things are going. He's found that people who are closed to Christianity are often open to prayer.

The key is not using prayer as a marketing technique, but caring for people and really believing that prayer can make a difference in their lives. I've known others who do the same thing through email. In the casual conversations they have with people, they'll offer to pray about issues that have come up: "That's a tough time you're facing. Would you mind if I prayed for you in the next few weeks?" Then they'll ask for an email address so they can follow up later in writing. They don't manipulate the conversation into a gospel presentation. They just genuinely care about the people they meet and want to pray for them. Often when people encounter another life crisis years later, they need to talk to someone. So they turn to the person they remember as safe, caring, and genuine.

I've found that when a relationship is deep enough to share the tough things of life, people are grateful to have someone partner with them in prayer. Unbelievers may not share your theology, but most are appreciative that someone with an "inside track to God" cares enough to support them.

Prayer is an effective tool in evangelism. If we are afraid to share or feel the pressure to steer every conversation toward the gospel, we can remember to pray for the people God brings into our lives. It means praying for people, asking God to work in each person's life and to make us sensitive to how and when we should share our faith with them. Then we pray that God will give us the strength, the courage, and the right words to say in the situation he has provided.

4. God uses us the way he made us.

God is fully capable of making turtles fly, but he doesn't. They're made to crawl, and are no less valuable than birds.

At five foot six, I've never had delusions of playing basketball in the NBA. I could spend my whole life working on my skills and practice hours a day. I could get really good at basketball, but it wouldn't make sense for me to make it my life goal. I'm designed to do other things.

I used to try to help my daughter with her high school math. To me it was simple—if I could translate a problem or equation into a real-life example (e.g., number of pieces of pie), it would make perfect sense. But those examples frustrated her. The more I tried to help, the more frustrated she became. She needed equations where she could just plug in numbers and make it work. Neither approach was better—they were just different. To this day, I use facts and figures to present my position to her.

In every area of life, God made us the way he did so he could use us in that way. The more we get in touch with our uniqueness, the more effective we'll be for the kingdom.

5. Satan does the opposite of what God does.

Satan is a deceiver, which means he tries to make us think something is true when it really isn't. Often he lets us believe about 90 percent truth and 10 percent untruth. That dilutes the truth just enough to make us ineffective.

If he can convince us that we need to share our faith in ways that don't fit the way God designed us, he robs us of the very tools God has given us to do his work. We get frustrated and give up. Satan has made us ineffective. (More on the work of Satan in chapter 9.)

So is everything we've been taught wrong?

No. It's just incomplete.

We've discussed the fact that a quiet personality is something to be celebrated, not healed. But we're living in an extrovert world with extrovert expectations. It's not comfortable to be a member of a minority, but it's one thing to know it intellectually and another to live it out daily.

So how does an introvert survive in an extrovert world?

5

form vs. function

Finding the Key to Guilt-Free Evangelism

I had never seen a church service start this way before—and haven't since.

The pastor stood before the congregation and announced, "We're a loving church, and we want you all to feel welcome. But we're also a biblical church. The Bible says, 'Greet one another with a holy kiss.' So stand up, turn to two or three people around you whom you haven't met, say hello, and give them a big kiss."

There was about one second of uncomfortable silence before the laughter started. People knew he wasn't serious—but it certainly got everyone's attention! I watched as people greeted each other: handshakes, occasional hugs, and a couple of kisses between spouses.

Later I thought about what had happened. Why were we so uncomfortable doing something the Bible specifically says to do? Was that really what the passage meant? If not, were there other passages we could ignore? How could we know? Did we have to pick-and-choose which commands of Scripture to follow?

The answer was pretty obvious. The emphasis in the command wasn't on *kissing* but on *greeting*. In the New Testament culture, a "holy kiss" was a perfectly acceptable, well-understood way of greeting someone. It wouldn't have raised an eyebrow in a first-century congregation. Today the injunction to greet each other still stands, but our cultural setting has provided different methods to carry out that greeting.

The greeting is a *function*—the basic thing that needs to happen. The kiss is a *form*—a method of carrying out the function. Much of our misunderstanding of Scripture today stems from emphasizing the form over the function.

Several weeks ago, I spent some time in a large local secular bookstore. The Personal Finance section was one of the largest sections in the building. As I looked through the shelves, I tried to count the number of titles that focused on getting wealthy. Some books had sensational titles, while others were more academic. Many dealt with investing techniques or various strategies, and others emphasized saving and budgeting. I stopped counting after I reached a hundred, because I was only about a third of the way through the shelves.

Suddenly I realized the common theme of most of the books: *we don't have enough money, and we want more.* This theme didn't say anything about methods for making money or whether the desire for money was based on greediness, ambition, or need. People wanted to improve their financial situations. Gaining wealth was the *function*. All the books had that theme in common. But their specific methods took different *forms*.

Was one book better than another? For different individuals in different situations, certain techniques are probably more appropriate than others. I might be immensely helped by one book, while the same resource would be meaningless to you. Why? Because you are not me, and your situation is different from mine. We might both want to improve our financial situation, but we will take different paths to make it happen.

Different Strokes

Several years ago, I spent some time in Ethiopia. I was traveling with Steve, who had been there many times before. He was teaching some local craftsmen how to build guitars, and I was assisting in the project. It was the first time I had been out of the country in thirty years, and it was reassuring to be on this trip with a seasoned traveler.

On the plane, he gave me some insight into the culture. We would be working closely with Yitbarak and Kassahoun, two warm, caring young men. He suggested that it wouldn't take long to develop close relationships with these godly men. "Don't be surprised," he said, "when they hold hands with you when you're walking together."

The more time I spent in the country, the more I came to appreciate the loving spirit of the people and noticed how physical they were with each other. It was hard to spot two people standing side by side who didn't have their arms around each other. When I was working on a guitar, they'd have their arms around me as they watched over my shoulder.

In Western culture, we tend to use less demonstrative ways to show our care for friends. So who is correct? The answer is reflected in an understanding of form and function. The function is to care about each other. The forms vary in different cultures.

I've been through a number of different classes and seminars on evangelism. Each had its unique approach and was designed to make it simple and effective for someone to share his or her faith with others. But like the books I found on evangelism, each seminar positioned itself as the newest and best approach. Each implied that its method would be easier and more effective than other methods. If it weren't, we wouldn't need a new technique when the others were just as good.

I remember one method that was clear and simple, but we had to memorize the process word for word. We learned how to steer a conversation around to spiritual things and then find a way to walk someone through the process. It was actually helpful, and there was security in knowing how to present the gospel in a logical format. But my problem wasn't with the technique. My problem was that we were supposed to use this technique in every encounter we had. Somehow that felt like the old approach of selling a product instead of providing a solution or like having your family doctor prescribe a medication without examining you.

The church has gone through different phases of evangelism over the years. The traditional approach, which emphasized the need to approach strangers and present the gospel, was popular for decades. It was characterized by door-to-door witnessing and confronting people on the street or in other public locations.

An alternative approach developed called "lifestyle evangelism," which was the subject of books, classes, and seminars. This focused on first building a relationship and then presenting the gospel. That meant we should take the person out to lunch first and *then* confront him or her with the gospel.

Because those approaches didn't fit the temperament of a lot of people, a third approach developed that's common today: *don't evangelize at all*. But that goes against the whole pulse of Scripture, because it focuses on forms while ignoring the biblical function.

It's easy to look at those methods of evangelism and find fault with them, assuming they have no validity. But they're just forms. God can use different forms with different people.

The important thing is to look at the *function* of evange-lism—*to bring people to the Savior*. All the methods people use are just forms to accomplish that function.

The apostle Paul got it right in Philippians 1:14–17. His Philippian audience was using different methods to share their faith, and they were accusing each other of using the wrong techniques. Some actually had the wrong motives and were sharing for selfish reasons. From prison Paul said,

- "Because of my chains, most of the brothers in the Lord have been encouraged to speak the word of God more courageously and fearlessly." (That's good.)
- "It is true that some preach Christ out of envy and rivalry . . ." (That's bad.)
- ". . . but others out of goodwill." (That's good.)
- "The latter do so in love." (That's good.)
- "The former preach Christ out of selfish ambition, not sincerely, supposing that they can stir up trouble for me while I am in chains." (That's bad.)

We might expect Paul to correct those who were preaching Christ from the wrong motives, but he makes an amazing statement in the next verse:

> But what does it matter? The important thing is that in every way, whether from false motives or true, Christ is preached. And because of this I rejoice.
>
> verse 18

Paul knew the difference between form and function. He might not agree with the forms being used, but he didn't really care as long as the function was being accomplished. The desired outcome was clear in his mind, but he knew God could take people on individual paths to get there.

On the Right Tract

When I was a young teenager, I wanted to share my faith, but I was too scared to do so. I had enough trouble holding a conversation with a stranger, much less engaging in an articulate presentation of my faith. Then I ran across a booklet with a title like "How to Evangelize Using Gospel Tracts." It suggested that if we left tracts in different public locations (phone booths, restrooms, bus stops, etc.), people would find them and read them. God could use them to convince the readers of their need for salvation, and those people would come to faith.

A few years later, I heard a speaker describe the technique he had developed for distributing tracts. He said that if he saw someone standing on the curb while he was driving, he could open his window, hold a tract at a certain height over the car, and release it at just the right speed so the wind would drop it at the person's feet. I was worried about being arrested for littering, so I didn't try it, but it reinforced my desire to give tracts a try.

I bought tracts and passed them out, praying that God would use them in the lives of the people who found them. It didn't feel quite like "real" evangelism, but it seemed like a step in the right direction. I eventually moved away from that method, because it seemed kind of impersonal. Plus, I *never* got to see what happened as a result of my efforts.

Later I heard that effective evangelism took place through personal relationships (whatever that looked like). Convinced, I decided that using tracts was not only ineffective but also wrong. They didn't grow personal relationships. I began to look down on people who used tracts. If I found a tract in an airport phone booth, I would think, *What a waste.*

But Paul's perspective began to haunt me—"What does it matter? The important thing is that in every way, whether from false motives or true, Christ is preached." God uses different methods with different people to bring unbelievers to himself.

If I minimize a form, such as distributing tracts, I might be minimizing the work God is choosing to do through one of his servants.

Paul's perspective has made me a lot more understanding of people who witness in different ways than I do. When I see a tract someone has left, I pray that God will bring it to just the right person. I don't expect people to read a tract and immediately drop to their knees, convicted of their sin, but God might use a tract in someone's journey to faith. The tract is just a form to help accomplish the function.

Do I use tracts now? Yes. I always keep at least one in my wallet, one in my planner, and one in the car. I don't distribute them randomly around the city. They're just available for me to give to someone as reinforcement if our conversation has led to spiritual things. It's especially handy if the conversation has been limited by time and a person has shown genuine interest.

Christian Bartending

In Romans 14, Paul presents the same perspective discussed above: "Who are you to judge someone else's servant? To his own master he stands or falls. . . . Each of us will give an account of himself to God. Therefore let us stop passing judgment on one another" (vv. 4, 12–13). While I must do what God has called me to do, I can't use that knowledge to criticize what others do. Otherwise, I risk criticizing God's work through that person's life just because it's different from his work through mine.

In one church where I was on staff, our minister of evangelism led a bartender to Christ. The man's daughter attended the church's elementary school, which was the point of contact between him and the church. His conversion was pretty dramatic, and he quickly grew in his faith and his love for his Lord. But he was still a bartender.

71

People in the church were excited but were waiting for the day when he would find a new job that was more in line with his conversion. One Sunday night, he had been asked to share his testimony with the congregation. He announced his plans to attend the local seminary and pursue studies in theology and psychology. The congregation was thrilled—until he said he was going to keep bartending. The reason? "Who do people share more openly with than their bartender?" he said. "I feel like God has put me in that position because people open up to me. I'm a good listener. But I want to study psychology so I can understand them and study theology so I have some answers for them."

The church almost split over that one. Many felt he was wrong to keep serving alcohol, because it would lead people deeper into their problems. Others thought it was a perfect fit, because he could reach people no one else would reach and he had already built their trust. The rest just thought it was wrong but didn't know why.

I don't think the debate ever got resolved, and I lost track of that man long ago. I'm still not sure exactly what I think about it, but I've learned a couple of things:

1. *It's between him and God.* No matter what I think, it's not up to me.
2. *We share the same objective.* The form will be different for different people in different situations, but the function is still to bring people to Christ.

Where the People Are

One of the reasons people seem resistant to the gospel is that they've become hardened to it. Through repeated exposure to inappropriate models that represent religion instead of a relationship with God, they've developed a type of immunity to faith.

They can hear about faith and watch it in people around them, but it doesn't seem to soak in, even though they need it.

That doesn't mean it's impossible to break through. It's just that the forms many Christians have used to present Christ tend to reinforce that immunity. We know it's important to find common ground with people, but our tendency is usually to try to get them to come onto our turf rather than to go onto their turf.

My sister sent me a CD of a couple of her pastor's sermons on evangelism. The pastor explained the importance of sharing our faith and issued a challenge to reach our circle of acquaintances who need Christ. For an action step, he asked each member of the congregation to write down the names of three people they would focus on in the next month. The goal, he said, was to find a way to invite them to church sometime during that month.

The problem is that while some people have found Christ in a church service, it doesn't always happen that way today. Except for seeker congregations, where the entire service is geared toward the non-churched individual, church is primarily a place for believers to come together for the functions of growth and encouragement. Then the church is supposed to disperse throughout the week, and each person lives in his or her particular slice of life. We figure that if we can get people into a church service, they'll be impressed with what they see (the forms) and the pastor can share the gospel with them. But from the perspective of our visiting friends, they're in a foreign country. The things we do in church aren't really common ground to them.

Think about it: Can you imagine going to work and standing side by side with your co-workers, holding hands and singing? Or having someone pass around a plate in which people put money (for something other than doughnuts)? Or in some cases, turning to a complete stranger and saying something religious that someone told you to say to them?

People don't need one more event to attend or one more cause to serve. If they want involvement in an organization, they have plenty to choose from. Church isn't always the highest on their list. If they are interested in spiritual things, they want a community of faith with people they like who are on the same journey.

If you were to go fishing, your goal would be to catch fish. So you put a hook on the line, hold the hook about a foot above the water, and whistle for the fish to come. "C'mon, fish. Here, fish. Come and get it." Would you get results? Probably not—you're trying to get the fish to leave his own environment, where he's perfectly comfortable, and come into your environment, where he can't breathe. There's no bait on the hook, and the hook isn't in the water. The fish has no reason to take you up on your offer.

If we want to catch fish, we need to put some kind of bait on the hook—a worm, a bug, something the fish likes. Then we need to put the hook in the water where the fish can find it. If the fish is hungry, he'll notice the bait and check it out. It's not our job to beat the fish with the bait; our job is to make sure the bait is in the water where the fish is. It's up to the fish to respond. The form has to be appropriate.

Finding common ground means we have to go where the fish live and live among them in an honest way. That's why it's important to rub shoulders with those who need Christ. We may be undergoing personal transformation, but it will be ineffective for evangelism if we're not close enough for anyone to see it. Most people would rather come to your house for a barbeque than spend Sunday morning in a church service.

Conversations with people in full-time Christian ministry reveal that many (perhaps most) do not have any significant relationships with non-Christians. It isn't much different with laypeople. A professor in an honors program at a large Christian university admitted that while the students learn how to think deeply about their faith, those students don't encounter many unbelievers while they're in the program. He found it was true for himself as well, even while leading the students in the program. That's why he and his wife have become actively involved in an animal rescue group—an area where they have personal passion—and get to build real, caring relationships with people who might not be interested in coming to church.

Norm Wakefield, author and professor at Phoenix Seminary, led a home church back in the '80s, when it was generally unthinkable to skip Sunday morning services. The group met for worship on Sunday nights instead. They found that it didn't usually work to invite people to a service on Sunday mornings, because that might be their only morning to sleep in, get up and go running, and hang out at the local bagel shop for an hour or two. For many, it was their favorite time of the week. Dressing up and going to church just didn't provide a suitable alternative.

So Norm's small "congregation" spent Sunday mornings running together and going to bagel shops for coffee. They would invite their friends to come with them to worship, and the response was amazing. They didn't look at their friends as projects. They just genuinely cared, got involved in their lives, and built relationships. As a natural result, the Sunday morning connection time brought more people to faith than most churches see in a year of services.

Of course, they had to put up with criticism from churches who thought it was improper to skip church on Sunday morning. Such churches thought the form was more important than the function.

We build relationships because we genuinely care about people, not just as a method to get them saved. Genuine care involves more than just their salvation. If we truly care about people, that care involves more than just their salvation. It involves every part of their lives, of which their spiritual health is one important part.

The Real Issue

Many people have wrestled with guilt because they feel disobedient to the Great Commission, but for quieter people, that guilt has come from an emphasis on form instead of function. Understanding the difference gives us a foundation for building a personal philosophy of sharing. We know God wants us to share. He has also provided whatever we need to carry out his will. Forms designed specifically for introverts will be much more effective for them than more traditional methods.

6

the fear factor

Figuring Out Why We're Afraid to Share
and Learning How to Harness That Fear

Fear has always been a factor in evangelism. Most people are hesitant to confront people about personal issues. Whether we realize it or not, we're all familiar with fear. Several different studies have shown that most people rate speaking in public as their greatest fear—greater than heights, insects, and even death (which is why most people would rather die than speak in front of a group).

The issues that make us avoid speaking in public are the same issues we face in evangelism: being the focus of attention, wondering how we're being perceived, saying the wrong thing and being embarrassed, and risking rejection for what we say. Notice the common characteristics of those items: the focus is on *me*. The best way to handle legitimate fear in speaking is to turn the focus outward—on the listeners and their needs. The more genuine our concern for other people is, the less impact fear has on us.

It's not easy to do, but it's possible. Usually our concerns about how others are responding come from our own minds—an inaccurate, incomplete perspective. We assume people are thinking the worst. When we learn to focus on what is *true*, our feelings become more accurate. Fear is best handled with truth.

What Are We Afraid Of?

Here are the ten most common fears about evangelism. They tend to be more prevalent in introverts than in extroverts:

1. How others are responding to us
2. Failure
3. Having people "see through" us
4. Not having the right answers
5. Having character flaws
6. Doing something we're not gifted at doing
7. Being embarrassed
8. Speaking to strangers
9. Getting tongue-tied and saying the wrong things
10. Getting "corrupted" by hanging out with unbelievers

Our bodies are designed to handle tough situations. If a car careens off course and heads straight toward us, we naturally feel a healthy fear. That fear enables us to quickly move out of the way for protection. So why does God say, "Do not be afraid"? Someone once observed that the Bible says "Do not fear" in 365 places—which would mean there's a different verse about trusting God for every day of the year.

The biblical perspective on fear isn't referring to our fight-or-flight reaction to stress. It's talking about not trusting God. Fear is the opposite of trust.

We can trust only what we know is true. Someone once said that faith is "trusting something you know is not true," but that's foolishness, not faith. True faith is only as good as what you place your faith in.

Fear often comes when we do something we're not wired to do. Suppose I get a call from one of the major television networks. "Our evening news anchor is taking next week off. We'd like you to fill in." My immediate response would be fear, and I would spend the next few sleepless days focused on how painful that opportunity would be. The network could say, "Don't worry about it—you'll do fine." They could tell me to have a positive attitude. They could tell me that other people have done the same thing and have been fine. But no matter what they said, I'd be afraid.

Is that fear wrong? I have to look at what is true. In this case, it's true that I'm not wired to be a network news anchor. That kind of fear keeps me from doing things I shouldn't do—like standing in front of a train, putting my life savings on a roulette table in Las Vegas, or delivering the national news. In those cases, fear is a signal that tells me to analyze what I'm doing and determine if I should be doing it or not.

But let's say a national newspaper or magazine calls and says, "Our front-page columnist is going on vacation next week, and we'd like you to fill in for her." Would I be afraid? No—I would be thrilled by the opportunity. I'd still lose sleep over it, and it would occupy most of my waking moments. I would have a healthy concern over the quality of my writing, but it would drive me to focus and perform.

That's the difference. When we do something we're not designed to do, fear tends to paralyze us and keep us from taking action. When we do something we are designed to do, we feel a creative tension that drives us forward.

Where does that fit into evangelism?

I've found that when I try to share my faith in unnatural ways, my fear gets larger and tends to stop me from sharing. That kind of fear almost always signals that I'm sharing out of guilt instead of compassion. But when I share in ways that fit with God's design for me, a creative tension compels me to look for new ways to move forward. Compassion drives me to look for unique, appropriate ways to make a spiritual connection.

The Upside of Stress

Ask a hundred people if they have stress in their lives, and most will say yes. Ask the same group if they'd like to get rid of that stress, and almost all will agree that they would. We know how we feel when we're under stress, and it's generally not a positive feeling. That's why people sign up for stress management seminars; they want to get rid of stress.

But they're called *stress management* classes, not *stress elimination* classes. There are different kinds of stress, and not all of them are bad. Hans Selye grouped them in two categories: distress and eustress.[1] The first, *distress*, is the kind that gnaws at our insides and causes headaches, ulcers, and ineffectiveness. The more of it we have, the more pain we feel. It impacts our physical, emotional, and psychological well-being and keeps us from enjoying the journey.

Eustress is the creative tension that helps us perform. Musicians, actors, and speakers recognize the power of eustress. Without it, they can't develop peak performance. Most professionals admit the tension they feel when preparing for a major presentation and value the edge it gives them. In fact, a performer who feels no creative stress will probably be limited in effectiveness.

It's kind of like a string on a guitar. There has to be a certain amount of tension on that string or it won't produce the sound it was designed to produce. If the string is hanging loose with absolutely no tension, it can't produce any music; if it's too tight, it breaks. The tension is essential, but it needs to be balanced.

The string produces a certain type of sound. No matter what you do to that string, it will always sound like a guitar. Someone might say, "But I like the sound of a saxophone. It's a better sound. You need to make that string sound like a saxophone." It's not going to happen. A guitar is made to sound like a guitar. A saxophone is made to sound like a saxophone. Neither is better than the other; *they both make music.*

In evangelism, we all have different "strings." Those strings won't play without tension—the kind of tension that helps us play perfectly in tune. That's the creative energy we feel when we're sharing our faith with someone we care about; it drives us to find appropriate ways to share. Fear is like putting too much tension on a string or expecting it to sound like another instrument. Our job is to discover what kind of instrument God made us to be and allow him to play through us. I might sound like a guitar; you might sound like a saxophone. If I try to sound like you, I have reason to be afraid: I won't be able to give a good performance.

But our goal is the same: we're both making music.

Praying for Boldness?

"But aren't we supposed to pray for boldness? Can't God do things through us that are outside of how we're wired?"

Chuck, a fifty-ish introvert, went on a short-term mission trip to India. The team was doing support work with an evangelist who was holding an evangelistic crusade in one of the major cities. When Chuck signed up for the trip, I don't think he was expecting to share his testimony before eighty thousand people. I'm guessing that when he was asked to do so at the last minute, he prayed for boldness. He probably doesn't remember a word he said that night, but it was a situation where God specifically called him to do something out of his comfort zone and then gave him the strength to do it. He didn't have to preach or sing or perform. He just had to tell his own story.

That's the exciting thing. God doesn't work *around* our weakness; he works *through* our weakness. Confidence comes from competence. Praying for boldness doesn't mean doing things we're not wired to do. It means asking God to work through us, helping us do the things he has called us to do. The important thing is to make sure we're doing what *God* has asked us to do, not what *others* have told us we should be doing. When God calls us to a challenging task, he doesn't expect us to work up the strength to do it. He provides the power to do what he's asked us to do. The power comes from God, not from us.

Some have suggested that Paul was an introvert because he prayed for boldness (Eph. 6:19–20), but everything we read about him suggests the opposite. As an extrovert, his prayer for boldness was a prayer for strength to do what God had asked him to do. His unique calling was to share the truth in the face of imprisonment and impending death. It would be easy to get distracted and discouraged by the threat of abuse, so he prayed for strength to stay true to his calling. He had to rely on God to speak through him, to give him the strength to say things that might be uncomfortable to say to that group. God had specifically called him to that purpose, and he needed boldness to share a message with a tough audience.

But I'm not Paul. If God specifically directs me to do something, it might be out of my comfort zone. Being bold means being willing to do exactly what he has asked me to do. Boldness might mean something different for an introvert than it would for an extrovert. It might mean writing an article and boldly saying things that touch nerves, causing people to think deeply. Is one type of boldness better than another?

Janice is an introvert, a professor at a theological seminary. She was in a class where I was leading a discussion of these ideas, and extroverts were commenting about the need to be bold in our witness. Most of the ideas had to do with talking—assuming that if God gives us boldness, he'll make us talk better. But in the middle of the discussion, Janice simply spoke four words that turned the entire discussion around: "That's why introverts write."

The extroverts in the group seemed reluctant to accept that writing is as legitimate as talking. But then the discussion shifted to influence. When someone talks to a large group, he or she might give a message to dozens, if not hundreds or even thousands, of people. But when someone writes, he or she has the potential to quietly spread the message to tens of thousands—even hundreds of thousands of people.

Years ago I wrote high school Sunday school lessons for a large interdenominational publisher. Once a quarter, the lesson would include a presentation of the gospel. The curriculum gave the teacher a specific way of presenting the message of faith to the class and included suggestions of how to meet the specific needs of the high school students. There was always encouragement for the teacher to pray deeply about the lesson before presenting it so that God would use the session to bring people to himself.

The curriculum was dated, so I always knew which Sunday the lessons were going to be taught. One Sunday I woke up and did the math. At that time, that publisher's curriculum was used in about sixty thousand churches in America. There was an average attendance in high school classes of about ten students. That means that before the day was over, I had arranged for the plan of salvation to be presented to around six hundred thousand high schoolers. Let's say that one student out of a thousand actually made a commitment to Christ that day—probably a conservative estimate. If accurate, it would mean that my lesson would have resulted in about six hundred people making a decision for Christ in one day.

So is talking always the best way to be bold? It would take me, an introvert, a long time to share my faith enough to bring six hundred people to Christ through talking. In writing those lessons, boldness meant I would include things that needed to be said, even if some people might criticize me for it. It meant taking the risk of approaching a publisher to write for them. Was fear involved? Not really, because I was doing what I was wired to do. But there was creative tension as I recognized the scope of my responsibility.

So will God give introverts the gift of evangelism? Absolutely. But they'll exercise that gift in unique, creative ways. They won't suddenly become extroverts; they'll let God work through their personalities. In fact, introverts have a unique advantage. They often recognize their inability to do it on their own, so it's more likely that they'll sense their dependence on God to work through them. They might be quicker to pray for strength and boldness in different situations based on that sense of need.

Freedom from Fear

So in a practical sense, how do we handle some of the common fears we have about evangelism? By answering them with *truth*. Let's look at the top ten fears related to evangelism and find the truth to counter each one.

Fear #1: *How others are responding to us*
Truth: Evangelism is God's work, not ours. When we share our faith, we often assume that people are responding to us, but they're really responding to God. When we use our unique gifts and temperament to share with others, we can trust God to handle their reaction.

Fear #2: *Failure*
Truth: God never asks us to be successful; he asks us to be faithful. When a person doesn't choose to respond to our message, that's his or her choice. We're not responsible for people's decisions. When we are faithful to do what God has asked us

84

to do, in the specific way he asks us to do it, we can leave the results in his hands. In her book *Woman, Aware and Choosing*, Betty Coble Lawther uses a tennis example: We're responsible for how we serve. We're not responsible for what the person on the other side of the court does with that serve.[2]

Fear #3: *Having people "see through" us*

Truth: Some of us often feel that others immediately know when we're faking it—trying to act confident when we're really trembling inside. But when we operate from the way God wired us, we're usually not trembling. If we're paralyzed by fear, we're probably doing something in a way God never intended for us to do it. When sharing is a natural expression of who we are, there's nothing for people to see through.

Fear #4: *Not having the right answers*

Truth: It's OK to say, "I don't know." Just because I don't know an answer doesn't mean the other person has "won." God is still working in that person's life. For example, I don't like to answer the door when someone of another faith is knocking. In that setting, they're generally operating from a mind-set of convincing others. (If someone comes to your door, intent on selling you a vacuum cleaner, you probably don't have a very good chance of selling them yours instead.) I know how much they've studied what they believe, and they know how to answer my objections. As an introvert, I usually think of things to say after they've left, so I don't put myself in situations where I have to debate people about religion—I'm not made to do that. There are other believers they'll meet who can hold in-depth discussions about theology. I've learned to be OK with that. But if I have the opportunity to build a relationship with someone of another faith, discussing spiritual things becomes much more natural. In that type of relationship, I don't have to have all the right answers. I can just love them and let God guide the conversation.

Fear #5: *Having character flaws*

Truth: We're forgiven, not perfect. Satan will try to convince us that we have no right to share our faith, because we haven't "arrived." But that's the point of salvation—it's an offer of forgiveness for imperfect people. The more human we are, the more people will be able to identify with us.

Fear #6: *Doing something we're not gifted at doing*

Truth: God made us just the way he wanted us to be, and he doesn't expect us to become something we're not. He might ask us to do something that's uncomfortable, but he'll also give us everything we need to do it. The power comes from him, not from us. We don't have to just try harder—we have to trust him for the strength. The key is to make sure he's the one who's asking us to do it. Otherwise, we'll be looking for strength to do the wrong task.

Fear #7: *Being embarrassed*

Truth: Embarrassment usually occurs in two ways:

1. *When we're focused on ourselves instead of on the other person.* If my motive for sharing is anything other than compassion, I shouldn't be sharing. I should pray for more compassion.
2. *When we're working outside our temperament.* If I'm not good at boldly confronting people with the gospel, I'll be embarrassed when I try to share. But if I'm gifted in this area, I won't worry about people's reaction.

People say, "Yeah, but it shouldn't bother us to be embarrassed. Paul was ridiculed and persecuted. Peter's life was threatened. Look what they did to Jesus!" But I'm not Paul or Peter, and I'm certainly not Jesus. If I felt like God was calling me to go through those things, that would be one thing. But the fact that God takes certain people on certain journeys doesn't automatically mean those same things apply to me. Yes, I can pray for boldness, but the boldness God gives me might be different from the boldness he gives someone else.

Fear #8: *Speaking to strangers*

Truth: Your mother was right: don't talk to strangers. For some people, sharing with a stranger is unnatural. It's one thing if God sets up a divine appointment and we sense his leading. Then we can trust him for strength. But in normal circumstances, introverts are made to share in the context of relationships. If I have the patience to develop a friendship, the time to share my faith will come as a natural part of that interaction. God's not in a rush, and his timetable is a lot different from ours.

Fear #9: *Getting tongue-tied and saying the wrong things*

Truth: When we trust God to work through us, people aren't going to be eternally doomed because we didn't give the best answer. Repeatedly in Scripture, when God says, "Do not fear," it is accompanied by, "I will be with you" (see Joshua 1). Sometimes we're so afraid of saying the wrong thing that we don't say anything at all. But God can use our words in those conversations, whether in person, in writing, or in an expression of love. Recognizing our limitations is also a reason to avoid situations where we have to give quick answers. A great reply is always, "That's a great thought. I'm not sure what I feel about it—let me ponder it for a couple of days, and I'll get back to you with my thoughts."

Fear #10: *Getting "corrupted" by hanging out with unbelievers*

Truth: We're told to be in the world but not of the world, but we've focused so heavily on the second part that we've avoided the first part. A recovering alcoholic would obviously want to avoid meeting people in a bar to share Christ with them, but that doesn't mean he or she couldn't meet people at Starbucks.

Scripture is clear on the need to engage unbelievers in relationships. The key is like a three-legged stool:

1. Stay close to God (for integrity and strength of character).
2. Stay close to unbelievers (for influence and relationships).
3. Stay close to believers (for accountability and partnership).

All three legs are important for the stool to remain balanced. Take one away, and you'll fall. Shorten one, and you'll always be wobbly.

Keys to Confident Sharing

- Recognize that God accepts us and uses us the way we are. We don't mind babies doing baby things; we accept the level where they are, knowing that growth is a process.
- Tell God when you're afraid, and ask for his help. He won't condemn you for it. Christ didn't rebuke the man in Scripture who said, "Help me overcome my unbelief" (Mark 9:24).
- Focus on loving others rather than on boldness in technique. "Perfect love drives out fear" (1 John 4:18).
- Ask God for boldness, but don't expect it to look the way everyone has told you it should look. Anticipate God's using who you are in powerful ways as he provides strength to do what he asks you to do.

7

the graceful witness

Becoming a Channel of God's Grace to People

I n my early years, I heard sermons about evangelism that focused on our responsibility to share our faith. The message was that if we didn't share, God was displeased. From that perspective, I began to feel that God was more concerned with my performance than with the people who needed him. Everything was based on guilt: if I didn't share every time I had the chance, I would feel God's wrath.

So what did I do? I shared my faith so God wouldn't be angry with me.

The problem was that I didn't feel a deep compassion for the people I was sharing with. Seeing God as an angry taskmaster shifted my focus from the people to the process. Little by little, I lost my passion for the people. They were just check marks in my mental evangelism log.

Most of us have experienced someone showing interest in us but later discovered that it was only because he or she wanted something. For example, our family bought a minivan a number of years ago. The salesperson spent about three or four hours with us one evening. We felt like we were the most important family he had ever worked with. He asked us about our interests, bought us pizza, and showed our kids a video of his bungee jump. We drove home in our new car. But the next morning, when I went back to sign a couple of additional documents, he didn't even remember my name or anything about our conversation. My attempts at a conversation were quickly dismissed, because the sale had already been finalized. He didn't really care about us; we were just a check mark in his monthly quota, and it was time to move on to the next prospect.

That's what happens when our evangelistic efforts are based on guilt. We become salvation sellers, with an emphasis on numbers rather than people.

A guest speaker at our church once made this statement: "We don't need more courage to witness to people; we need more love." He described how we use courage when we're in threatening situations, and it focuses internally—on us and our techniques. But the more we love people, the more we will want to share with them. The focus will be external—on them, not on us. We won't have to convince people of what they need; they will come to trust us as we deeply care about them as whole people.

That's evangelism based on grace, not on guilt. But many believers have been taught this guilt-based approach. As a result, their compassion for people often decreases rather than increases.

Jesus had stern words for those who made the methods more important than the people. When the Pharisees criticized Jesus for healing someone on the Sabbath (which was against their rules), Jesus pointed out that they would rescue a sheep who fell in a pit on the Sabbath and that a man was more valuable than a sheep. "Therefore, it is lawful to do good on the Sabbath" (Matt. 12:12). The person was more important than the ritual.

The whole New Testament emphasizes God's grace. He doesn't require us to be perfect; if we could do that, we wouldn't need salvation. Instead, he asks for faithfulness where we are right now. "It is required that those who have been given a trust must prove faithful" (1 Cor. 4:2). There are no strict requirements to do evangelism in a certain way (form). Our responsibility is to walk closely enough with God to see what he's doing and then to be sensitive to how he wants us to partner with him in that situation.

For example, we're often told that God gives strength in weakness (2 Cor. 12:9)—so we're supposed to go out there and be bold, and God will work through us. There are two problems with that perspective. First, it assumes that to have strength means to be outgoing and forceful. Second, it puts the responsibility on us to *act* tougher, when the passage says it's something God does through us. Not only that, the passage doesn't say our weakness turns into a strength. It says that God works *through* our weakness. Paul is describing the thorn he possessed—something that seemed to get in the way of his ministry. But God didn't take the thorn away; he used it as a tool for ministering grace into the lives of others.

We're still the same people, with the same unique wiring, but God uses that wiring to express his strength through us. The advantage? It's obvious to everyone that God is doing the work, not us.

The Bilingual Christian

I speak English—period. I took two years of German in high school, but I only remember two sentences: "I can't find my overshoes" and "I must buy myself a new jacket." I've tried to work them into casual conversations but haven't found many opportunities. I've often thought I'd like to go back and take more classes in German, since I have at least a foundation in the language, but I really don't have that many German-speaking people in my life.

During my visit to Ethiopia, I learned a few important phrases in Amharic, such as "hello," "thank you," and "bathroom," but I'd be hard-pressed to hold a conversation. If I really wanted to communicate with someone in that country, I would need a translator—someone who knew both languages well.

As believers, our role is that of translator. We speak one language (faith), and non-Christians speak another (unbelief). Since they don't speak our language, they won't understand anything we say no matter how articulate we may be. They've never experienced faith.

Our goal is to be bilingual. We've experienced belief, so we speak that language. If we've come from a background of unbelief, we know that language as well. If we've been raised in an environment of faith, we may not know the language of unbelief—but we need to learn it. We need to know both languages, but our communication has to be in unbelievers' "native tongue" if they're going to hear the message.

We don't have to convince most people of the validity of our arguments—we just have to use our lives and our words (spoken, written, or otherwise) to translate the truth into terms they understand. If someone speaks "introvert," they're generally not going to be reached by someone who speaks only "extrovert." They don't know the language and will usually be impacted more by a fellow introvert. That doesn't mean extroverts can't reach introverts and shouldn't try to share the gospel with them. It means extroverts need to learn the basic introvert "language." How do they learn? In the same way marriage partners learn about each other—spending quality time together to learn each other's unique views on life.

Terry once confided that since he had grown up in a solid Christian home, he couldn't identify with unbelievers. He felt like he didn't have anything to say, because he couldn't even remember his life before Christ. "I don't have a glowing testimony," he said. "Maybe I should have killed somebody or something." In other words, he felt he didn't speak the language of unbelievers.

Yes, he knew a language they didn't—a language of grace and protection—and had the gift of a godly heritage, but just because he hadn't been brought up with their experience doesn't mean he couldn't connect with unbelievers. He just needed to learn their "language" by spending time with them, developing relationships. That doesn't mean steering initial conversations toward the gospel. It means building a genuine connection with another person, sharing in his or her life and building a trusting relationship. The relationship is characterized by patience, so God is free to work in the friendship as it grows.

I go into different corporations on a daily basis. Every company has its own culture, but there's one thing I find almost every time. As I wander through the rows of cubicles and offices, people have pictures of family and loved ones, items that have special meaning to them, and even posters of sports figures they admire tacked to the walls. They're trying to bring a sense of their values and priorities into their work space. In fact, you could probably spend five minutes in a person's cubicle and have a pretty good idea of what is important to him or her.

An extrovert might look at these cubicles and say, "These people need Christ. Let's get them all together and share the gospel." That's probably exactly what an extrovert would do (assuming God has directed him or her to do that). It fits his or her personality type. But introverts won't see the room full of cubicles; they'll see the pictures, plaques, and posters in a single cubicle and say, "This person needs Christ. I need to get to know him better and learn about the people in these pictures. If I learn what's important to him, I can find out where Christ might fit in his life." Two different approaches, and both effective in the right circumstances.

In one hotel where I frequently present seminars, the young man who sets up the audio-visual equipment for me is becoming a friend. We get to talk only once every two months or so, and it's only for about ten minutes at the beginning of the day. I haven't shared the gospel with him yet, and I don't know when I will or what it might look like, but I keep track of what he's involved in and ask him about things we talked about the last time. He appreciates my interest in his life outside the hotel job, including the band he plays drums in. We've talked about his future plans and where music might fit into his life. I'm not forcing my faith, just building a relationship.

I drop in enough casual comments to position myself as a person of faith, so he knows where I'm coming from. That's setting the stage for the time when the conversation might move toward spiritual things. In the meantime, we're talking about music. It's not my favorite style of music, but I could drop by the coffeehouse where he plays on weekends to build the connection.

Some people have implied that I'm shirking my responsibility. "What if he gets in a car accident tonight and gets killed? Won't you wish you had shared your faith with him?" Probably. But I'm responsible to God to do what he leads me to do in each situation. I'm confident that I'm not the only one God is bringing into this young man's path. God is using a variety of people and circumstances to draw this young man to himself. His response isn't my responsibility, but my faithfulness to follow God's leadings is my responsibility.

For years I've taught life management skills to secular audiences. Since I'm representing a company, I can't overtly present my faith in that setting. I can drop in hints so people know where I'm coming from, but I can't suggest spiritual solutions to their issues. That used to bother me; I wondered if I was doing more harm than good, since I was giving people solutions that would give them more control over their lives and less stress—but without God. Was I actually diminishing their pain so they wouldn't sense their need for God?

Fred heard my concerns over coffee one day. I respect his opinions more than most people's, because he's a gifted evangelist working full-time in evangelistic ministry with the Navigators. His response: "Don't worry about it. You get to stand in front of fifty or sixty people a day and get them to think deeply about what matters most in their lives. Most of those people haven't done that for years. Don't you think God can take what you've set up and use it to lead them through the next step in their spiritual journey?"

I shared that perspective with my wife, who has observed me in full-time professional ministry for the first half of our marriage and secular work for the other half. Her comment: "You have more of a ministry now than you did when you were *in* the ministry." I think it's true. I don't spend as much time as I used to trying to present the gospel, but I'm seeing more people move closer to God because of my interaction with them.

As Rick Warren said in *The Purpose Driven Life*, "It's not about you."[1] Grace means that God chooses to use imperfect people to carry out his work. He's not limited by my performance. Leading someone to faith is a team effort, even if we don't always see what the other members of the team are doing.

Going for Grace

So how does grace give us freedom to share that we don't have under guilt?

- It lets us work in our unique gifting and temperament.
- It assumes that God is the one doing the work and that he's using us in the process.

- It recognizes that our job is to build relationships; God's job is to use those relationships to bring people to himself.
- It allows different people to use different methods of sharing their faith.
- It emphasizes the need to stay close to God so we can see where he wants to use us and how he wants us to respond in each situation.

Disobedience doesn't come from ignoring the techniques we've been taught; it comes from ignoring the voice of God when he moves us to do something in a specific situation. Grace allows us to relax and let God work through us in his way, in his time, and in his strength.

8

what would jesus do?

Discovering How Christ Interacted with People

I've often wondered what it would be like if Jesus were physically living in our society today. Everything we read about him took place in the first century, when the culture was much different than it is today. To really understand how he lived, we have to understand first-century culture. But how would he live today?

- Would he hold big crusades?
- Would he make TV appearances?
- Would he drive a car? If so, what kind?
- What kind of neighborhood would he live in?
- What would he do for recreation?
- If he were chosen for a reality show, would he get voted off the island?

- Would he watch football on TV?
- Would he need a PDA to keep track of his schedule?
- What methods of evangelism would he use?

Some might consider these questions sacrilegious, but the issue goes back to form and function. When we look at the way Jesus lived, we're looking at form—the things he did that were appropriate in his culture. But there was nothing sacred about the form. It was just a way of carrying out the function.

I really don't know the answers to any of these questions. I know he would be passionate about carrying out the functions that were important to him, drawing people to himself. I'm guessing he would choose some forms that might surprise us. After all, the religious leaders of his time (the Pharisees) were upset about his methods. He broke the religious rules to accomplish his ministry: healing on the Sabbath, hanging out with the wrong people, touching the unclean, and so on. He did things "spiritual" people thought were inappropriate, but he was more concerned with the function than the form.

I'm not immune to this "spiritual" thinking. Even though I know better, I am sometimes surprised to hear a well-known pastor or Christian leader express passion about a particular sports team. Something inside tries to tell me that a dedicated leader would be beyond such casual interests and would certainly never pay good money for season tickets. But then I remind myself of the truth—we're more than just spiritual beings. Besides enjoying participating in an area of strong interest, a leader will also be connecting with many more people because he or she shares common ground with them.

We've heard it told that Christ walked everywhere he went, and we assume he'd do the same today. But in the first century, walking was the primary means of transportation. I don't know what he'd do today, but it wouldn't surprise me to see him using modes of transportation that are common in our culture. I'm not sure if he would own a car or just ride with others, but because of his passion for people, I picture him always having someone along for the ride, living his life in proximity to other people.

Would Christ hold big evangelistic crusades today? The best answer is maybe—or maybe not. The feeding of the five thousand didn't seem to be an organized event. Lots of people simply gathered as they followed Jesus, and he took the opportunity that presented itself. Does that mean Billy Graham and Greg Laurie are wrong for filling stadiums to preach the gospel? No, because God has led them to use that form. In our culture, God has used men and women to reach mass audiences with the gospel. Most Christians know someone who came to faith in Christ in one of those large-scale meetings. God hasn't asked everyone to use that form of evangelism, but he has chosen some to do so.

Would Christ use television or radio to deliver his message? Personally, I have trouble seeing him with a weekly show. But since, in our culture, the media is so much a part of people's lives, I'm guessing he would find a way to use that media. If his first-century pattern of breaking religious rules applied, he probably would appear on more secular stations than religious ones.

Focus on Function

Rather than guess what methods Jesus might use, let's focus on the functions. Based on our previous discussions, we can assume two things:

1. He wants to impact people's lives eternally.
2. He uses whatever methods are appropriate to make that happen.

What does eternal impact look like? If we look past the forms of Jesus's first-century ministry, we can focus on three primary functions:

1. He ministered to people he encountered while going about his daily life.

There are a few instances of Christ moving directly toward someone who needed a divine touch, but reading through the Gospels, we see him primarily spending his time with the Father and then spending time with his disciples. His focus was to teach the disciples and develop a sense of mission in them. As he did that, he encountered people throughout each day. When he did, he stopped and met their needs.

2. He met people where they were and moved them one step closer to God.

Jesus never seemed to be in a hurry to present the gospel. Time after time, he met people exactly where they were in their life situation, identified their need at the moment, and took steps to meet that need. Sometimes that involved bringing them to the point of making a decision for God. Other times it involved their need for physical healing, emotional care, or a challenge to their lifestyle. Whether encountering his disciples or the general public, Jesus's goal was the same—to love people and move them a step closer to knowing God.

3. He prayed for God to minister through him.

Jesus didn't meet everyone's needs while he walked on earth. He was involved in full-time ministry for only three years, and he left many needy people behind. Yet near the end of his life, he prayed, "I have brought you glory on earth by completing the work you gave me to do" (John 17:4).

It seems strange that Jesus had to pray, since he was God, but he was also fully human. Philippians 2 tells us that he "made himself nothing, taking the very nature of a servant, being made in human likeness." Even though he was completely God, he put himself in the human position of depending on God to work through him. In everything he did, he relied on the Father to do it through him.

His philosophy of evangelism seemed to be, "Love people and talk to them."

Twenty-First-Century Application

Most of the methods (forms) of evangelism presented today are based on the functions Christ demonstrated. People who employ those methods have a desire to bring people closer to God, and God has used them to impact the world for Christ. However, those methods might not suit our personalities, so we would do well to study the functions Christ focused on and find unique forms to carry them out.

1. We can minister to people we encounter while going about our daily lives.

Jesus was a master at turning ordinary encounters into supernatural appointments. We read of him eating, walking, following the cultural traditions, sleeping, praying, and conversing with his friends. As he wandered along the dusty roads, he built object lessons around the common situations he encountered—fig trees, fields ready to harvest, a restless sea. We don't see him sitting his disciples down, setting up a PowerPoint presentation, and lecturing them on theology. He simply lived his life in proximity to their lives. They learned by living close to him.

That type of instruction is infinitely more time-consuming than a classroom setting, but the impact is multiplied. Through that life-on-life process, the disciples learned how to love the people they encountered and to see them through eyes that searched for their needs.

"But that takes too much time," you say. "I already have enough on my plate without having to share my faith as well. When will I work that in?"

Most people today are busier than they would like to be. This is reinforced by a society that values productivity. When evangelism is seen as an event, it becomes one more item on a long to-do list. People look for opportunities to check things off and then feel more accomplished.

Would Jesus be that busy if he were here today? The key was that he was busy about the right things. His priority was the preaching of the gospel (what God had called him to do—Mark 1:38), primarily in synagogues and villages where instruction like that took place. Pick a few chapters in the gospels, and we can trace the pattern. As he went about his life, people came to him. When they did, he knew that God had arranged these encounters, and he took time for them. Look at the number of people just in the first three chapters of Mark who came to Jesus rather than him initiating the encounter:

- The man with an evil spirit cried out to Jesus (1:23).
- Jesus went to Simon and Andrew's home and healed their mother during the visit (1:29–31).
- People brought needy people to Christ (1:32–33).
- A leprous man approached Jesus for healing (1:40–42).
- A paralytic man's friends brought him to Jesus (2:3).
- Religious leaders engaged him in dialogue (2:16–17).
- A man with a shriveled hand found Jesus in the synagogue (3:1).
- Crowds followed him from around the region (3:7–8).

Jesus knew what God had called him to do (preach the gospel) and made it the focus of his energy. But as he carried out his ministry, he was available to the people the Father brought into his path.

That's a freeing concept. First, we need to be close enough to God to know specifically who he wants us to be. Then as we live our lives, being who he created us to be, we can be open to the people who come into our path. Our role is to be available to respond to needs as they arise, in the way that we're wired to meet those needs. We also don't have to meet every need that's out there—just the ones God puts in our path.

2. We can meet people where they are and move them one step closer to God.

Over the past few decades, many churches have convinced their members that evangelism is an event rather than a process. But Jesus didn't treat it that way. If he followed the pattern of many churches, he would have found a way to turn every encounter into a formal presentation of the gospel. Instead, we see him meeting people in everyday situations, talking to them about exactly where they were at that point in their lives, and edging them forward to the next level of belief. In each conversation, he wasn't distracted; he was totally focused on the person in his presence.

I'm learning the necessity of being totally present for the people God brings into my path. I don't know what God is doing in another person's life. If I'm distracted, or thinking about something else, or wondering how that person perceives me, I'll miss the chance to learn where he or she is in his or her life. But if I look at each encounter as a God-arranged opportunity, I'll be sensitive to what God wants to do through our conversation. If God is using our connection to bring the person closer to himself, I need to listen to find out where he or she is right now. It means more than just good eye contact; it means getting my focus off me and onto the person in my presence.

3. We need to pray for God to minister through us.

Ask believers if they think prayer is important, and they'll agree that it is. But if they were to keep a minute-by-minute log of how much time they actually spend conversing with God in prayer, it would probably be a lot less than they would expect.

Some time ago, I decided to pray for ten minutes a day. It was OK if I went over the allotted time, but I made sure I prayed for at least ten minutes. At first it seemed like an artificial exercise, but after a few days, I noticed how powerful that time was. That realization showed me how little I actually prayed. I thought about it and talked about it, but I didn't spend much time doing it.

Jesus prayed often, asking God to do things through his life. What made me think I could be effective on my own? When I tried to figure out evangelism, it was frustrating, but when I started praying for people who needed Christ, I saw God set up supernatural encounters. I didn't have to force spiritual issues; I just responded to what God was doing. Sometimes that would move the conversation toward spiritual things, sometimes not. But I learned that praying for someone had much more power in a person's life than my attempts at steering a conversation in a certain way.

The bigger task for us is to abide in Christ—spend real, focused time with him to have his power in our lives. Then he'll be free to work through us in the lives of others.

Evangelism by Listening

I'm also learning the power of listening. Careful listening accomplishes three things: First, it puts my focus on the other person instead of on me. Second, it builds trust with the other person, since he or she knows I'm not just pushing the gospel but am genuinely interested in his or her situation. Third, it helps me learn where God is working in that person's life, so I can join him in moving that person to the next level.

People aren't used to being listened to. In most conversations, we're used to the posturing that takes place when each person is trying to make the best possible impression on the other. When we don't feel understood or listened to, it's like being trapped under the ice on a frozen lake, desperately needing to find air. Until we get a breath, nothing else matters.

When we listen to people, we give them the air they desperately need. If we jump into a gospel presentation before we give them air, they won't be ready to hear it. But if we take time to listen, we build trust in the relationship. They know we're not just looking for spiritual scalps; they know we care. That caring is "quick to listen, slow to speak" (James 1:19). Someone has suggested that God made us with two ears and one mouth, which should indicate the proportion we should be using each part.

When we're focused on our own agendas, we miss the richness that comes from truly listening to another. Charles Simmons, a motivational sales trainer from the 1950s, wrote a small booklet titled "How to Get a College Education Every Six Months." He suggested that other people have knowledge and experience we don't have. If we can set aside our agendas and actively listen, we'll learn something new from each conversation. Seeing other people's perspectives helps us understand them better, providing more opportunities to explore common ground in conversations.

Most people listen only in order to respond. If we truly learn how to approach conversations with a mind-set of listening and understanding, we'll gradually earn the privilege of sharing. It allows God to bring people to himself through us.

Tips for the Timid

It's always good to pattern our choices after the choices Jesus made, but some of his choices were simply forms that reflected the culture he lived in. If we're going to follow his example, we need to follow his *heart*—make current-day choices that reflect the things that were important to him rather than just his methodology.

So what would Jesus do?

- He would pray.
- He would ask the Father to bring the right people into his life, and then he would respond to them. He would love people.
- He would be intentional but patient about guiding people toward faith.
- He would take time with people to explore their needs.
- He would communicate with people.
- He would be himself.
- He would look at people through God's eyes.
- He would allow God to work through him.
- He would listen.

Should we do any less?

9

what would satan do?

Learning How Satan Keeps Us
from Sharing Our Faith

In 1896 Charles M. Sheldon wrote *In His Steps*,[1] in which he told the story of a man who lived his life by asking, *What would Jesus do?* In every situation he encountered throughout his life, this question was the filter through which he made choices. When the book rose in popularity again a few years ago, it spawned a line of WWJD products, such as bracelets, key chains, and bookmarks. Everywhere you went, people were wearing WWJD as a reminder to ask themselves what Jesus would do in each situation they encountered throughout the day. It wasn't an evangelistic tool, but it helped people live their lives in the context of God's will.

I didn't have a WWJD bumper sticker, but I thought the idea was great. Along with other people, I found value in the constant reminder to consider God's perspective on my life issues. There is another perspective that could be just as powerful, though it is generally neglected: *what would Satan do?*

I don't think they'd sell many WWSD bracelets in Christian bookstores. But if we ignore the tactics of our enemy, we'll be at a huge disadvantage in the battle. While sports teams spend hours practicing and perfecting their skills, they also study video footage of their opponents before playing against them.

It's important to learn godly responses to life situations, but it would be foolish to ignore the strategies of Satan. We have "footage" available to study, both in Scripture and through the lives of people who have fallen prey to him. What can we learn from watching Satan's past performance?

- We're in a real battle, and Satan is our enemy (because he's God's enemy).
- He knows he won't win in the end, but he doesn't want us to know that.
- He wants us to keep fighting but to do so ineffectively.
- If we're ineffective, his soldiers won't defect to God's side.
- He's in the battle 24/7.
- He wants us to be ineffective in the battle 24/7.

What would happen if we lived our lives with both perspectives?—*What would Jesus do?* and *What would Satan do?* We would be strengthening both our offense and our defense for the battle. As believers, we're called to be engaged in both positions. We need to understand the strategy of our enemy "in order that Satan might not outwit us. For we are not unaware of his schemes" (2 Cor. 2:11).

So What *Would* Satan Do?

1. He would keep us distracted.

Several years ago, I was walking through the crowded *mercado* in Addis Ababa, Ethiopia. I had been warned that pickpockets were everywhere in this open-air marketplace and that I should empty my pockets before walking there. In the back pocket of my jeans, I replaced my wallet with a New Testament that was about the same size. I figured if someone stole it, at least he or she would get some *real* value out of it. Then I headed off for the marketplace.

Because I had been warned, I was especially sensitive to what was happening around me, so I was aware of a man walking toward me but facing backward as though he were calling out to someone behind him. We were on a collision course, and I moved to the side, but he still bumped my shoulder firmly, then stopped and apologized profusely, grabbing my arm in the process. Suspicious, I reached for my back pocket and found another person's hand pulling out the New Testament.

Initially I hadn't even realized it was happening.

Later I was discussing the incident with others and learned that it was a common technique. One person sets up the distraction, which makes the victim temporarily unaware of the crime taking place. Pickpockets know it's impossible to focus on two things at once.

It happens in every area of life. In Southern California, we hear daily of traffic accidents caused when people become distracted by seeing an accident and rear-end the car in front of them in the process.

The apostle Peter says, "Be self-controlled and alert. Your enemy the devil prowls around like a roaring lion looking for someone to devour" (1 Pet. 5:8). It takes self-control to stay alert. Why would Paul tell us to stay alert? Because it's easy to get distracted. If Satan can get our eyes on something other than what he's doing, we'll give our attention to what seems urgent instead of what's important.

Satan often uses the issue of methods to distract us. If Satan can convince us that certain techniques of sharing our faith are the only legitimate ones, he'll convince us to chase after them and distract us from what God designed us to do. We'll be ineffective in the battle, because we'll be using somebody else's tools and techniques. Plus, we'll be focused on our frustration, since the methods don't seem to be working, and we'll be distracted from the immediacy of the battle.

2. He would keep us divided.

When I was a teenager, one of the common pranks played in our high school parking lot was to open the hood of someone's car, switch two of the spark plug wires, and close the hood. Then we'd hide and watch the unsuspecting driver try to start the car. (Of course, I never participated in the prank—I only watched.) The car owner's efforts were futile. It was such a small thing when you consider how many thousands of parts have to work together to make an engine perform, but if the wires are crossed, the car simply can't do what it is designed to do.

The human body is the same way. If I have a headache, my entire body is affected. I can have the greatest intentions to be productive, but if my head hurts, my mind, feet, and hands fail to perform. That's why Paul spends so much time explaining to the Corinthians why they need to be unified in their efforts. "The body is not made up of one part but of many. . . . Those parts of the body that seem to be weaker are indispensable. . . . So that there should be no division in the body. . . . If one part suffers, every part suffers with it" (1 Cor. 12:14, 22, 25–26). Satan had divided them against each other, and the impact of the gospel was compromised.

Jealousy and pride can make us ineffective. If I look at your gifts and compare them with my own, I can become jealous and feel inferior. I'll be inclined to not use my gifts.

Satan will try to divide us from our fellow soldiers, encouraging us to work independently instead of as a team. If he can divide the army, he can make them ineffective. If we spend our time fighting over the forms, we'll be unable to carry out the functions.

3. He would keep us deceived.

When we're deceived, we think something is true when it really isn't. That's what's so dangerous about deceit—we don't realize it's happening. We're told that Satan deceives the whole world (Rev. 12:9; 20:10). As residents of this world, we're not immune. Satan will do whatever he can to convince us that something is different than it really is. He often shows us something that's *close* to the truth to keep our focus away from what is *completely* true.

For example, he tries to convince us of his power. When we see so much evidence of depravity and godlessness in our society, it's easy to believe that Satan is winning and God is losing. If that's true, we would have reason for throwing in the towel. It's true that Satan is powerful, but it's also true that God is infinitely more powerful. Focusing on Satan's power can limit our effectiveness, because we're focusing on the wrong thing.

If we had spiritual vision that enabled us physically to see where Satan is working around us, we would probably be surprised at how frequently he is involved in our everyday lives. But if that same vision allowed us to see where God is working, we would see the truth of the battle. Elisha's servant was frightened when he saw that they were surrounded by the enemy's army of chariots and horses, but Elisha prayed that God would open his eyes.

> "Don't be afraid," the prophet answered. "Those who are with us are more than those who are with them." . . . Then the LORD opened the servant's eyes, and he looked and saw the hills full of horses and chariots of fire all around Elisha.
>
> 2 Kings 6:16–17

Satan doesn't care if we share our faith as long as we're ineffective in doing it. He tells us our methods aren't legitimate or effective or even biblical. He tries to convince us that we need to witness like other people do, which robs us of the very gifts God gave us to use in sharing our faith. If we're using somebody else's methods, we'll be ineffective. Or in most cases, we'll give up sharing our faith altogether.

4. He would keep us discouraged.

When my dad taught me to mow the lawn, he always had me pick a spot at the far end of the yard that was exactly where I wanted the lawnmower to go. Then as I pushed the mower, he had me focus on that spot. "Don't look at the lawn," he'd say. "Look at where you want to end up." I'd usually do what he said, but sometimes I couldn't help myself. Halfway across the lawn, I would glance back to see how I was doing. Inevitably, when I reached the other end, the crooked line showed me exactly where I had taken my eyes off the goal.

When I was finished, the lawn might have looked great, but all I could see were those two or three places where I had messed up. By focusing on the mistakes, I was discouraged and felt like a failure. But I wasn't noticing the huge areas that had been mowed perfectly.

Discouragement is looking back at what has gone wrong rather than focusing on the destination. Literally, *discouragement* means to take the courage out of someone. Satan loves to focus our attention on the process, pointing out the futility of our efforts. But God often tells his people to be strong and courageous. It's not something they just have to work up or something they have to pretend. We can be courageous because of his presence. "I will be with you"—that was his promise to Joshua when he asked him to lead the children of Israel into the Promised Land:

> Be strong and courageous. Do not be terrified; do not be discouraged, for the LORD your God will be with you wherever you go.
>
> Joshua 1:9

Satan tries to convince us that we're alone in our efforts. If we try to share our faith in our own strength without God leading us, we have reason to be discouraged. But when we share in the way God designed us to share, and we recognize his presence with us, we'll gain the courage to do what he wants us to do.

Ten Ways Satan Sabotages Our Sharing

1. He tempts us (Matt. 4:1).

If Satan can convince us to sin, we'll feel unworthy to share our faith. We'll think, "What do I have to say to unbelievers? I'm no better than they are." *Solution*: People aren't attracted by our perfection; they're brought to Christ because of his mercy, grace, and forgiveness.

2. He schemes against us and outwits us (2 Cor. 2:11).

Because Satan is a deceiver, he knows our weak spots and goes after them. It's like playing chess: he has watched us long enough to know our patterns and can guess our next move. *Solution*: We need to study his moves as well and be keenly aware of his patterns. Then we'll be able to more accurately guess his next move—or at least recognize it when it happens.

3. He appeals to our pride (Matt. 4:8–9).

Satan has been around long enough to know that people want to be liked and respected. If he can convince us that witnessing might make people dislike us or look down on us, we might not do it. *Solution*: Being sensitive to the reactions of other people can help us build trusting relationships where sharing becomes a natural part of a sacred companionship.

4. *He lies (John 8:44).*

In fact, Satan is called the "Father of lies." Just as we can trust God to be truthful, we can trust Satan to be untruthful. He often presents something as absolute truth but dilutes it with 10 percent untruth. But whether it's 10 percent or 100 percent, Satan lies. Lying is his native language, and it's easy to be caught up in his lies. *Solution*: The best way to recognize counterfeit money is to become thoroughly familiar with real currency. In the same way, as we become more and more familiar with God and his truth, we'll be able to recognize anything that's different.

5. *He works on our hearts (Acts 5:3).*

Satan knows that our emotions and passions are found in our hearts, so that's where he attacks. Just as advertising targets our emotions to get us to respond, Satan targets our hearts to get us to do what he wants us to. *Solution*: "Above all else, guard your heart" (Prov. 4:23). A guard is someone who is paid to protect something valuable, taking action as needed when an enemy approaches. Anything as valuable as our emotions and passions deserves to be guarded from intruders.

6. *He convinces us to become friends with the world (1 John 2:15).*

Satan's strategy is to make the things of the world as attractive as possible. That's why it's often hard to resist. You wouldn't let your toddler play with a razor blade just because it was bright and shiny. In the same way, an inappropriate relationship with the world compromises our impact. *Solution*: We're told to be actively engaged with the society around us but not to love the world or the things that are in the world. We need to constantly remind ourselves of the reality of God's plan for the world and our part in that plan.

114

7. He engages in battle with us (Eph. 6:11–18).

The stakes are high; Satan is fighting for our lives. Besides the subtle ways he tries to trip us and trap us, he makes a full frontline assault against us. If we're not aware that a battle is taking place, we can be wounded and not be able to fight—thus making us impotent in our battle with the enemy. *Solution:* We need to understand that a battle is taking place. To fight effectively, we need to put on the whole armor God provides. We're vulnerable without the armor, and we're foolish to fight without it.

8. He masquerades as an angel of light (2 Cor. 11:14).

If Satan presented himself as darkness and evil, it would be obvious who he was, and it would be easier to resist him. But he disguises himself. On the surface, we may think we're encountering a messenger of God himself, but it's a trap, and it's easy to fall for outward appearances. *Solution:* The more we know God, the more we'll be able to spot an impersonator. "Do not believe every spirit," the apostle John says, "but test the spirits to see whether they are from God" (1 John 4:1). It's important to look closer than first impressions.

9. He looks for opportunities and takes them (Eph. 4:27).

Satan doesn't take a vacation. He knows our humanity better than we do, and he watches for us to open the door a crack for him to work—and then he rushes in. If he can get his foot in the door, he has the chance to influence our lives and our witness. *Solution:* We need to realize the impact of small decisions that can give Satan a foothold. The closer we walk with God, the more we'll recognize inconsistencies that Satan can take advantage of.

10. He interferes with our ministry (1 Thess. 2:18).

We've all watched sporting events where a player tries to break the rules behind the referee's back. Satan breaks all the rules, interfering in anything we do that carries out God's work. *Solution:* God, the referee, has already disqualified Satan—but

Satan hasn't left the court yet. So we need to be aware of his tactics and pray for God's intervention to protect his work from Satan's interference.

So Is There Hope?

When Christ died and rose again, Satan was declared the loser—but for now he's still in the ring. If we live in the truth of Christ's victory, we can share in that victory with him. But since the battle is still raging, it's important to know the tactics of the enemy "in order that Satan might not outwit us. For we are not unaware of his schemes" (2 Cor. 2:11).

Satan is somewhat predictable, since he's been using the same methods for a long time, but he targets those methods to specific individuals. He'll do anything he can to keep us from sharing our faith effectively.

Yes, there is hope for all of us. It's found in James 4:7—"Resist the devil, and he will flee from you." That's what Jesus did in the wilderness. It wasn't immediate; in fact, Satan tempted him for forty days. But at the end of that time, "the devil left him" (Matt. 4:11). Resisting the devil means learning how our enemy works and taking offensive and defensive measures to render him ineffective.

Asking *What would Jesus do?* and *What would Satan do?* can give us a balanced perspective on sharing our faith.

10

methods that are biblical

Developing a Truly Scriptural Approach to Evangelism

Just because some believers have given up on evangelism doesn't mean they don't want to share their faith. Because of the way they've been taught, sharing just seems foreign to the way they're wired. So rather than become something they're not, they simply lower the priority of evangelism to manage the guilt of not doing it. The reasoning: *if it's not that important, then I don't need to feel so guilty about it.*

But if we spend any time in Scripture, it's hard to get away from God's passion about bringing people to faith. If we're going to be biblical believers, we must share that passion. But being biblical is about functions, not about forms. It means having God's desire to guide people toward faith but doing it through the unique methods he has given us.

I've watched believers find great freedom in sharing their faith in the ways God designed them to share. When we become biblical witnesses, we can become passionate again about bringing others to Christ. That passion comes when our focus is on the function instead of on the method.

So What Does It Mean to Be Biblical?

Fortunately, Scripture is filled with examples of God's use of a person's uniqueness to do his work. We can find encouragement from studying the same passages that have produced guilt in the past.

Second Kings 7 presents a simple picture of evangelism. It's the story of four men with leprosy who are dying because of a famine. The whole city is starving, and these men come up with a plan. Since there is no food, they know they're going to die, so they decide to go to the enemy camp and surrender. The worst that can happen is that the enemy will kill them—but since they're going to die anyway, they haven't really lost anything. There is also a chance that the enemy will let them live, perhaps as prisoners. In that case, at least they will be able to eat.

When they reach the enemy camp, no one is there. It seems God has used fear to drive the enemy away from their camp. They left so quickly that they didn't take anything with them—clothes, food, and treasures. Suddenly the four lepers can feast on the supplies they find, and their lives are saved.

But the people in their native city are still starving. One of the men finally makes the connection:

> We're not doing right. This is a day of good news and we are keeping it to ourselves. . . . Let's go at once and report this to the royal palace.
>
> 2 Kings 7:9

118

The city officials don't believe the men at first, but eventually they check out the situation and find it to be true. God has emptied the enemy camp so the people in the city can survive. The famine is over.

But if the four lepers hadn't reported what they had seen, they would have lived while the city perished.

That gives us a simple, biblical definition of evangelism: *one beggar telling another beggar where to find food.*

The Imperfect Witness

Somewhere along the line, we got a strange idea about how to live in front of unbelievers. Many Christians have been taught that we have to appear *perfect* to the world, or at least close to it. After all, Christ is supposed to change our lives—make us new creations and make all things new. Others should be able to look at the changes in our lives, which will make them want to follow Christ so they can have the same kind of change in their lives. If we don't appear perfect, people won't be impressed with the changes.

That perspective sets up two major problems. First, it implies that if people follow Christ, he'll make them perfect and take away all their problems. It's true that trusting Christ puts people in the *position* of being perfect, meaning they are forgiven by God's grace even though they're guilty of sin. But if they have the expectation that their lives will become perfect, they'll be set for a pretty hard fall.

Second, that perspective assumes people will be more attracted to a lifestyle that's perfect than one that is flawed but forgiven. But people can't identify with perfection; they know only humanity. They need to see someone who is just like them, with all their warts and emotional wrinkles, who has been forgiven by God and empowered to live their life. When we appear to be perfect, people feel we're setting ourselves above them, judging their morality and lifestyle.

I spent years trying to hide my humanity. I didn't want people to know if I was angry or discouraged or anything less than victorious. I tried to crawl up on a pedestal so others would want to come up there with me, but I found it put me out of their reach. They saw where I pretended to be and assumed I couldn't identify with their place in life. Humanity is exactly what people need and respond to.

It's good that the apostle Paul never tried to present himself as someone who had arrived. If he had, we would read his exhortations and say, "Yeah, easy for you to say. You're the apostle Paul. You've got it all together." The reason we benefit from his example is that he was still in process:

> What I want to do I do not do, but what I hate I do. . . . I have the desire to do what is good, but I cannot carry it out. . . . When I want to do good, evil is right there with me. . . . What a wretched man I am!
>
> Rom. 7:15, 18, 21, 24

We read those words and say, "Yeah, that's me! He sounds just like me!" We feel that Paul is demonstrating his humanity, and it makes us want to sit up and take notice of what he says.

That's why it's healthy to be an imperfect witness. The Bible never offers instant perfection when we believe. Instead, it describes the lifelong growth process of becoming more like Christ. We're not saved from every problem; we're given his strength to face them, his presence to walk with us through them, and his patience to help us grow in the midst of them.

People aren't attracted by our methods; they're attracted by our lives. So the most important basis for evangelism stems from who we are on the inside. *Being* is a prerequisite to *doing*. It starts as an inside job.

I might believe some powerful truths, but if those beliefs are only in my head and don't impact the way I live, nothing about my life will draw others to faith.

People live tough lives. They want to know that Christ offers something that can impact the issues of their lives, and they look to us to see what that something is. If my beliefs don't impact *my* life, unbelievers won't see a reason for those beliefs to impact *their* lives.

Introducing Mutual Friends

It isn't our job to force people into the kingdom. Evangelism doesn't stem from a sales model, where we structure the conversation to close the deal. Most of us have had experiences where someone has pressured us into a purchase we really didn't want. Even though we purchased the item, we probably didn't use it and decided we would never do business with that salesperson again. He or she had pressured us to buy something we weren't ready to buy.

I need to replace my garage door. I don't know a lot about garage doors, so I've started doing some research. I heard an ad on the radio that offered a garage door at the "lowest price in town" from the "best dealer in the state" (that's what they said about themselves). I went to their website and will probably visit their showroom, but I also went to a couple of other independent websites for information on what to look for in garage doors. Last night, having dinner with three other couples, I asked if any of them had any experience with garage doors. Dan had recently replaced his and explained his choice of vendor and his experience with that company. Because I trust Dan, I'll be investigating that company.

After I've done my research, I'll know what I'm looking for and which vendor I'll choose. At that point, if a salesperson from that company happens to come to my door selling his services, I would probably buy from him. That person would probably leave my house thinking, *I'm a great salesperson. I just walked up to the door, and convinced him to buy my product*, but really he got the sale because I had done my research and already knew my purchase would be from that company. If someone from another company came to my door, he wouldn't make the sale.

As Christians, we're not salespeople; we're just introducing mutual friends. When I have two friends I care deeply about, I naturally want them to know each other. I introduce them and share the good qualities I know about each one, hoping they'll appreciate each other as much as I appreciate them. I can't force them into a friendship, but I know how much each of them means to me and want them to experience the quality of that relationship as well.

Of course, we all know of people who dislike each other on the first meeting but eventually become friends. When that happens, it's their own decision. We can be there as a sounding board and help them think through their feelings, but it's their decision. Our job is to make the introduction.

Evangelism is the same way. Our job isn't to force people to believe in God. Our job is to introduce our close friends to each other. Even the terminology we use fits that model: we *lead* people to Christ or *introduce* them to the Savior. We make the introduction, then act as a sounding board as they discuss their feelings about their initial encounter with God.

That's a freeing concept for believers who've never thought about it that way before. Sensitive, caring people don't want to force someone into a decision he or she isn't ready to make, but introducing one person they know well to another Person they know well can be a natural progression of a relationship.

David Benner says, "We follow a person—Jesus. Jesus does not tell us where to go; he simply asks us to follow Him."[1] He talks about the importance of introducing people to Christ rather than having them follow our path. We don't prescribe their journey for them; we simply make the introduction, encourage the relationship, and then let it develop along its own lines.

Pictures of Persuasion

Scripture provides several metaphors of evangelism for us to draw from. When we're compared to salt, light, and seed, the examples all center on *influence* rather than control or coercion. For some believers, influence is the primary tool God has provided to impact the world around us.

From each metaphor, we can derive unique characteristics to apply to the process of sharing our faith.

Salt—"You are the salt of the earth" (Matt. 5:13).

- *Salt comes in little pieces.* Unbelievers will be impacted more by multiple encounters with believers than by conversations with one person. It's a team effort, and we're part of the team.
- *Salt preserves.* Our involvement in a non-Christian's life can keep him or her from making a wholesale commitment to Satan.
- *Salt causes thirst.* Motivational speakers often say, "You can lead a horse to water, but you can't make him drink. But you can salt the oats."
- *Salt brings out flavor.* Salt should enhance the flavor of whatever it comes in contact with. If the correct amount has been added, we don't taste the salt; we taste more of the flavor.
- *Too much salt hinders growth.* When sprinkled in the soil, salt can keep things from growing. When consumed by humans in large quantities, it can cause illness or death.

Light—"You are the light of the world. . . . [People] put [light] on its stand, and it gives light to everyone in the house. . . . Let your light shine before men, that they may see your good deeds and praise your Father in heaven" (Matt. 5:14–16).

- *Light radiates outward.* Christ is the source of light (John 8:12).
- *Light draws attention to another object rather than to itself.* We don't see the light; we see the objects the light shines on. We're called "light" in Scripture, which means unbelievers shouldn't focus on us. Rather, our light should make it easier for them to see God.
- *We notice light only when it's absent.* Commander Richard Byrd, after six months in a metal hut at the South Pole, said, "I find that I crave light as a thirsting man craves water."[2] In the daytime, a single match goes unnoticed, but light the same match in a pitch-black cave, and it's obvious throughout the whole cave. Those of us who feel ineffective with typical ways of doing evangelism have a huge impact by simply being lights in front of people living in darkness.
- *Light is silent.* When people are lost and in the dark, light is a welcome gift to show them the path out of the darkness. When an introvert is lost and living in darkness, a fellow introvert with a flashlight needs only to shine it on the exit. No instructions are needed; if that person is ready to escape his or her situation, he or she will go for the exit when it becomes visible.

Seed—"The seed is the word of God" (Luke 8:11).

- *Seed grows without our help.* Mark 4:27 says, "Night and day, whether [a man] sleeps or gets up, the seed sprouts and grows." We can plant it, and someone else might water it, but God is the one who causes growth.

- *Different seeds work in different conditions.* Not everybody can reach everybody. God designed us to be effective with certain people.
- *Seeds need well-prepared soil to germinate and grow.* Some encounters with unbelievers may be preparing the soil; others may be planting seed, cultivating, pulling weeds, or harvesting. But until someone has prepared the soil, the seed probably will not take root.
- *Not all planted seed will germinate.* The parable of the seed and the sower describes the factors that can keep seed from growing and taking root (Mark 4:2–20).

How to Live in the World

Columnist Jonathan Rauch said that atheists care as much about religion as evangelicals do—just in the opposite direction.[3] I've learned that most believers attack atheists or other people who hold strong opinions against faith. The common approach is to equate them with the enemy and allow those who are good at making strong defenses of faith engage them in debates.

We're Christians, and our identity is in Christ, but we're also total people with life concerns, bills to pay, and child-rearing challenges. Our faith permeates our whole lives, but if someone relates to me only in matters of faith and ignores the rest of my life, I don't build a strong relationship with them.

Atheism doesn't entirely define a person either. Atheists are normal people who don't believe in God. We forget that they have mortgages to pay, kids to raise, challenges at work, and health concerns. I've learned that I can have a close relationship with people who believe differently than I do. I don't ignore their beliefs, but those beliefs don't form the basis of our relationship. I find them to be people whom God loves and cares for deeply. In that kind of relationship, we know our differences in belief, so it's not an untouchable area. They won't come to faith primarily by my arguing my position (which I'm not wired to do anyway). God will draw atheists to himself through people who care and build relationships with them.

When I was teaching in a Christian university, I noticed how supportive the Christian community was when students wanted to go into full-time Christian service or missionary work. But if a student changed majors from ministry to broadcasting, it was seen as a few notches down on the Christian career ladder. I don't minimize the value of Christian ministry in the least and am deeply committed to the work of missionaries around the globe, but think of the impact the secular media has on our society through television, movies, and print journalism. If God called someone to that field, he or she would have a tremendous opportunity to make an impact on the world. That person generally wouldn't be able to change the entire direction of a company, but he or she could build relationships with the most influential leaders in our society—leaders whose only contact with Christians comes through boycotts and antagonistic protests.

Larry Poland caught that vision years ago as a pastor of a growing church. God gave him the opportunity to develop caring, personal relationships with some of the most influential leaders in Hollywood. He didn't approach them to witness. He approached them simply to build friendships and offer to pray for them. Many of these leaders said they had seen thousands of Christians angrily protest, boycott their organizations, and sign petitions, but no one had ever bothered to talk to them or build a relationship with them. Years later Mastermedia International has helped thousands of people catch the vision of sharing instead of shouting, of praying instead of protesting. The result?

God has used that gentle, common-ground approach to soften the attitudes of many media leaders toward faith.

In order to meet people where they are at any given time, we need to get close enough to them to find out where they are. God will show us the needs of the people he brings into our path.

Generally, people are more receptive to God when they're not in control. A good friend who has the gift of evangelism works in a hospital with families going through crisis. She doesn't try to share her faith with people who are in control. They won't be receptive at that time. She stays close enough to them to see when something happens that causes their control to crumble. When something happens to cause people to lose their sense of security, such as a financial collapse, a terminal illness, or a wayward teenager, they become more receptive to God.

People have an innate sense of God whether or not they realize it or admit it. It's usually during a time of crisis that they reveal that sense. When the Twin Towers fell on September 11, the most common expression heard on television throughout the day from terrified citizens was, "Oh, my God." They didn't swear or logically express their concern. They didn't say, "Wow" or "I can't believe it." Those comments came a little later, but the first words from their lips were an instinctive acknowledgment of God.

A few years ago, an atheist was interviewed here in California on one of the local news programs. The topic had to do with an event that involved the separation of church and state, and he had been called in as an authority on the topic. While he was describing the need to keep religion out of society, an earthquake took place. The studio was visibly shaking, and people were ducking under the news desk. In midsentence, the atheist stopped briefly, then said, "Oh, my God—it's an earthquake." Not exactly the phrase he had planned on saying, but it came out instinctively.

People have "earthquakes" in their lives occasionally, when things move unexpectedly. At that time, they often begin to question everything else in their lives too. It's during those times that they'll be more receptive to what God wants to do in their lives. Who will they discuss their fears and concerns with? The people who have cared about them deeply enough to build trust.

The workplace is a good example. Many people are ineffective witnesses in their places of employment because they've presented a less-than-accurate example of what a Christian is. Putting up Christian posters in our cubicles, keeping our Bibles open on our desks, and forcing coffee-break conversations to spiritual topics isn't the place to start. Christian witness in the workplace begins by being the best worker possible to gain the respect of management and co-workers. Once that has been accomplished, trust develops. We can build relationships with fellow employees based on the common ground found in our daily tasks. When that happens, people will be able to see how Christians respond differently to the frustrations and challenges that come up in the workplace. When they encounter life situations where their usual set of responses turns out to be inadequate, they'll turn to the people who handle it differently to see if they have different tools.

Sharing by the Book

Fred Wevodau of the Navigators once told me, "The kingdom of God is advanced by the spiritual transformation of ordinary people living among the lost." If we're not being spiritually transformed, we won't have an impact on anybody. Even at the end of Paul's life, he said he had not yet reached perfection and God was still transforming him (Phil. 3:12–17).

That has practical application for all believers, no matter what our personality type. If our lives are genuinely being transformed through Christ's power, others will notice. They'll notice how we talk to our spouses during phone calls at work. They'll notice how we talk about our spouses in front of others, building them up instead of tearing them down. They'll watch our reactions to the tough situations we face and will see how we handle the positive situations as well. If what we say is different from what they observe, they'll always believe what they observe.

Being a biblical witness involves exactly that—being. Someone noted that we're called human beings, not human doings. The deeper an introvert's relationship with God is and the more it grows, the greater the impact he or she will have on others. When we become salt in our society, light in the darkness, and seed for sowing, God will use our efforts to bring people to himself.

11

techniques that are personal

Customizing an Approach That Is Uniquely Yours

Years ago I saw a display by the checkout register of a local bookstore. It was a series of booklets designed to teach you how to bluff your way through life. Each small booklet was designed to provide, in a few minutes, just enough knowledge and buzz words about a particular topic that you could hold a conversation about it with someone. There were booklets to help you talk about things like golf, football, the stock market, sales, and marketing. You didn't really have to know the subject; you just needed enough terminology and understanding of basic concepts to *appear* to be knowledgeable. The result? Social survival. If you knew you were meeting with an avid golfer, you'd be able to talk about handicaps, bunkers, and greens without thinking about blue parking spaces, army shelters, and vegetables.

At first I was offended by the idea of learning just enough to fake it in a conversation, but the more I thought about it, I realized that the basic concept was just what I needed. One of the biggest challenges some of us face is knowing how to keep a conversation moving. Usually we participate in a kind of verbal dance, testing out different topics until we find one where we share common ground. That's the basis for starting and growing any relationship. I don't want to bluff my way through a conversation, pretending to know things I really don't, but there's value in learning a little bit about a lot of topics in order to find a starting point for connecting.

I'm not an expert in everything. I don't have to fake it, but it's good to learn a little about a lot.

Developing Your Own Style

Few people would classify themselves as absolute extroverts or absolute introverts. Most of us are somewhere in between, often depending on a specific situation. That's why a one-size-fits-all approach doesn't work. Let's look first at some basic principles that apply to everyone. Then in the next secton, we'll explore some specific suggestions we can use as ingredients in our own recipe for success in sharing.

1. Recognize that God's strength is demonstrated by using our temperament, not by changing our temperament.
Every kid playing basketball has a model to which he or she aspires. Throughout the '90s, most kids tried to be like Michael Jordan. They would practice his shots and try to emulate his every move.

That gave them a base to build their skills. But as their skills developed, they would grow into their own unique style based on their physical build. Instead of following Michael Jordan, they would study the style of veteran players who were closer to their body type and physical structure.

Eventually, their own unique approach would develop. They could still learn from watching others but would focus on their own giftedness more than on copying the style of others. Shaquille O'Neal never tries to play basketball like Michael Jordan. Why? Because he's not Michael Jordan. He knows that his strength on the court comes from maximizing his unique strengths and capabilities, not from trying to be someone he's not.

David was expected to fight in Saul's armor but was able to defeat Goliath only by using his unique abilities in his own way. He credited God with the victory when the battle was done.

Our society tends to value productivity. We're used to quick solutions: "Just give me five easy steps, and I'll do it." But each person is unique, and God works through each of us individually and uniquely.

2. Understand that we're players on a team, and each of us has a unique role.

When a sports team wins, every player says, "*We* won." Even the players who sat on the bench share the victory. In the actual game, teammates work together to set up the shot for the person who scores.

Imagine what would happen if you had

- an orchestra with fifty flutes and nothing else
- a fruit salad with only bananas
- a restaurant with only cooks and no servers
- a company with only managers and no workers
- a newspaper with only editors and no reporters, printers, or delivery people
- photographs with light and no dark
- a recipe whose only ingredient was flour

When Austin came back from fighting in Iraq, I asked him what he did there. On the surface, his computer skills might seem rather unimportant compared to frontline combat, but his job was to program the trajectory of missiles. If the missile hit the target, it was because Austin made it happen. I'm guessing his fellow soldiers understood the value of his contribution more than we do.

Tom does lighting for the film industry. While the focus of public attention is on the actors, he's the one who makes them look good. We'd have to sit a long time in a theater at the end of a movie to see his name roll across the screen, but without his contribution, the success of the movie would be jeopardized. During the awards shows, we get only a brief report of the behind-the-scenes awards. We never see the actual presentations.

First Corinthians 12:17, 22–23 describes God's purpose in designing people uniquely:

> If the whole body were an eye, where would the sense of hearing be? If the whole body were an ear, where would the sense of smell be? . . . Those parts of the body that seem to be weaker are indispensable, and the parts that we think are less honorable we treat with special honor.

Every part (every personality type) is needed to accomplish God's work.

3. Learn what you need and find ways to meet those needs.
Joni Eareckson Tada has described her passion for ministering to the physically challenged and has a relentless drive to increase the impact of her ministry around the world. But she also knows her limitations. In one poignant interview, she described the reality of being a quadriplegic and how much time it takes her caregivers to meet her basic needs. She also talked about what happens when she drives herself too hard and doesn't take the time to give herself what she needs. She

has learned that if her unique needs are not met, her ability to carry out her work diminishes.

Introverts need time to recharge, and that usually happens when we're away from the crowds. The more introverts are involved with other people, the more critical it is for them to find time alone. The key to living in an extrovert world is to be consistent in taking time to recharge. If we don't take that time, we can lose our effectiveness and eventually burn out.

4. Set boundaries.

This comes from point number two above—knowing our unique role on the team. If we understand that God made us a hand, it's easier to resist the pressure to function like a foot. When we know we're going to be in an environment that drains our energy, we need to take time before the event to build up that energy. During the event, we need to give ourselves permission to take breaks, spending a few minutes alone outside to refuel. Knowing our limits gives us the freedom to leave the event before others do.

The most effective way to say no to pressure is to have already decided what our boundaries are. It's not being mean or antisocial; it's simply understanding our needs and clearly thinking through how those needs can be met.

If I run out of gas on the freeway, my car won't run. So when I notice the fuel gauge approaching empty, I need to stop for gas. It doesn't matter how busy I am, or how late I'm running, or how frustrated I am at the price of gas. If I don't stop, the car will simply stop running. In the same way, I have to pay attention to my emotional fuel gauge. If I see symptoms that I'm approaching empty, I need to take steps to recharge.

5. Learn to stretch.

Introverts and extroverts can each use their temperament as an excuse for who they are. "I'm a quiet person," the introvert says. "I'm just not good around people."

But God didn't make us this way to avoid others. He specifically gave us our temperament *to be involved with others*. The purpose of our design is to be intentionally involved in the lives of others. They need what we have to offer, and we need what we can get only from them. Paul said, "The body is a unit, though it is made up of many parts; and though all its parts are many, they form one body. . . . There are many parts, but one body" (1 Cor. 12:12, 20).

There's nothing wrong with working on our interaction skills, as long as we're not trying to become something we're not. Introverts need to learn how to function alongside extroverts when they're in extrovert territory. Some people are happy being introverts and need to learn how to capitalize on that when interacting with others. Other introverts don't like their quiet side but need to learn how to use it in social situations.

Start by finding out who you are, how God wired you, and learning to accept and even celebrate that. Then learn how to use that wiring, taking baby steps outside your comfort zone.

How Do I Start?

No matter what our temperament, we need to look at different areas of life through the lens of our own wiring. Here are some examples:

- *Writing*—Extroverts often accuse those who use email extensively of hiding behind their computers instead of having face-to-face conversations. But for some people, email is a tool, not a crutch. They communicate more effectively through writing than they might in a conversation. It's not weaker for them—it's actually stronger. Writing gives introverts a chance to carefully think through their words before delivering them.

- *Taking time to think*—Have you ever walked away from a conversation thinking, *I should have said this* or *Why didn't I reply this way?* Since some people process information internally instead of aloud, they often feel bad because they don't think quickly on their feet. They regret the things they wish they had said but couldn't think of at the time. It's not a sign of weakness; it's just that they're uncomfortable during the interaction. It's healthier to say, "I'm not sure how I feel about that. You make some good points; I need to take some time to think about what you've said. Let's talk again in a couple of days, and I'll give you my reaction."

- *Dealing with impatience*—"But my co-worker won't wait around for a couple of days to hear my answer," you say. That's possible, but it doesn't mean you need to be pressured into responding before you have something to say. There's no biblical principle that says that you have to win every discussion, especially when it's happening. Bob, an extrovert, will be challenged during a lively discussion with another extrovert. Phil, an introvert, might be challenged by the comfortable pace of another introvert's deep thinking. If Bob and Phil hold a conversation, Phil can still provide thought-provoking input to Bob—it'll just happen a couple of days later, and maybe in writing.

- *Building relationships*—Meeting new people can be hard for some introverts. Sometimes a different approach helps. When I'm going to have a first-time conversation with someone, I'll often email ahead of time to build rapport. Then when I have a live conversation, there has already been a point of contact. When I make connections within my comfort zone, it gives me a base to stretch a bit outside that comfort zone. At social functions, I can take the initiative to approach others who look lost or uncomfortable (they're easy to spot if you're an introvert, and you'll often find them alone on a balcony getting some space).

When I'm leading a seminar, I usually try to meet the participants ahead of time, asking their names, occupations, what brought them to the seminar, and so on. I've gotten pretty comfortable with this process, because I'm the one in charge. I assume people will talk with me, since they know I'm leading the class. If I were just a participant, I wouldn't approach anyone in the room. I've always thought, *They wouldn't want to talk to me.*

At one seminar, I had introduced myself to about fifty or sixty people, when I saw a woman whom I hadn't met standing at the refreshment table. I approached her and introduced myself, and she responded enthusiastically. We talked for three or four minutes, and I was thinking how easy it was to converse like this when I was the leader of the group—people automatically responded. Then she said, "And what do you do?"

I was speechless for a minute as I realized what had happened: she didn't know I was teaching the class. I had approached a stranger who didn't know me and had initiated a conversation, and she had responded. It wasn't because of my position; it was just the result of one person approaching another.

That was a turning point for me. It challenged my perception of myself as a person people might not want to talk to. I realized that day that my perspective is generally inaccurate. People respond to genuine interest from others, whether the person is in charge or not.

Switching from Sales to Customer Service

One of the keys to connection with others is finding common ground. When people shift away from contrived approaches, sharing is a natural by-product of common-ground relationships. The focus shifts from sales (what I want you to know) to customer service (what you feel you need).

People are turned off by high-pressure sales techniques. We tend to do business with people we like and trust—people we believe are genuinely interested in us and care about what we need. The faith-sharing techniques that fit our individual personalities can't be used simply as canned methods. They become a set of tools that are used as needed in the course of caring about another person.

When my wife and I bought our first house back in the '70s, we were excited to own something instead of just paying rent each month. It soon became apparent, though, that ownership included maintenance. Things needed repair, and we had no landlord to call. We had to do it ourselves.

In those days, we had very few tools. We pounded nails with our screwdriver, trimmed bushes with a pocket knife, and measured the size of a room with a foot-long ruler. We didn't enjoy the process because we didn't have the right tools.

Over the years, we've managed to collect many tools, so when a job needs to be done, it's a lot easier and much more enjoyable. The more tools we have, the more options are available for finding the exact one to do the job well.

That's why techniques are important in sharing our faith. If we have only one or two canned presentations, we'll try to make them fit every situation, but if we've developed a collection of resources, conversations about faith become easier, more effective, and more enjoyable.

So how do you collect tools? Here are some possibilities:

- Read the front page of each section of the newspaper each day. It won't take long, but you'll be able to participate in discussions about the day's current topics related to news, sports, business, human interest, and weather.

- Observe the details of the environment around you. On an airplane, for example, I usually make a comment to a seatmate about the crowdedness of the plane, the temperature, or the lateness of the takeoff, or I ask if the person is coming home or going somewhere. I don't have to run a whole conversation, but it's just enough to touch on common ground. If the person carries the conversation further, I can simply respond. I find it easier to respond to someone else's conversation than to initiate one myself.

- Ask people about their families. Whether they have toddlers or teenagers, they probably have some stories to tell. Don't try to give advice; just listen empathically. That usually takes a conversation beyond surface talk pretty quickly.

- Everyone knows something you don't. Explore a little, and then ask for their perspective. You don't have to agree, and you don't need to force the conversation in a certain direction. Approach it with a genuine interest in learning what they know. They'll appreciate your interest and be more receptive to discussing things that interest you later.

- Make sure you have one or two hobbies, areas of interest or expertise, or organizations you participate in. Learn them well; it will provide a launching pad for numerous areas of common ground with others.

- Listen. A lot. Don't feel pressured to respond; just listen. If you think of things you want to say, bring them up later or email your ideas to the other person. But for now just listen. It's a great tool for finding common ground.

- Read *How to Win Friends and Influence People* by Dale Carnegie. It's been around for years but gives practical advice for handling the give-and-take of relationships.

- Practice being confident with who you are. Listen to what you're telling yourself during conversations, and

140

learn to sort out truth from fiction in your perception of yourself.

- Realize the value of eye contact (introverts usually have good eye contact when listening but not when speaking).
- Ask open-ended questions to allow others more chance to talk and to give you more time to listen.
- Experiment in your next conversation by focusing on one thing: learning the person's name.
- Listen more than you talk. When you listen carefully, people remember you as a good conversationalist.
- Assume you have something to offer—that you can somehow encourage other people and that they'll feel better after talking with you.
- Don't steer the first conversation with someone toward faith (or politics). Make the first encounter one of relationship building and finding common ground. That will set the stage for faith conversations in the future.
- Ask people questions about themselves: where they live; where they're originally from; their job, training, background, and interests. Don't use these questions as a technique; focus on genuinely wanting to know them better.

A Great Verse to Remember

One of the most freeing verses in the Bible is Colossians 4:6:

Let your conversation be always full of grace, seasoned with salt, so that you may know how to answer everyone.

Whether our temperament is outgoing or more reserved, it was designed by God. He wants to use us the way he made us.

This verse shows what our responsibilities are in sharing, no matter what our personality type.

- Stay close to God.
- Be gracious when interacting with others.
- Have "flavorful" conversations, no matter what form they take.
- Think through how you would answer people ahead of time.
- If you don't know how to respond, say you'll think about it and get back with the person (and then do it).

I'm writing this chapter in a coffeehouse. A few moments ago, my dentist (an extrovert) came in. I see him for about two minutes twice a year after the hygienist cleans my teeth. Though he couldn't remember my name, he recognized me and walked over. We talked for about five minutes. I didn't try to share the gospel with him; we talked about golf. Having noticed the collection of golf balls and tees decorating his office, I simply stepped into a conversational area of interest to him, and he seemed surprised that I remembered.

Did I fail because I didn't bring the conversation around to faith? I have extrovert friends who would say yes. But while those same friends might quickly engage my dentist in a discussion about theology, they probably wouldn't have noticed his interest in golf. For me, our conversation strengthened our relationship a bit and strengthened a foundation that might grow in the future.

Next time I see him, he'll remember our brief encounter today. And if he finds coffee stains on my teeth, he'll remember where he saw me getting them. God is fully capable of advancing the conversation from there. From teeth to golf to coffee to . . . ?

The more I become "me," the more effective I'll be in sharing my faith with others.

12

intentional sharing

Restoring Our Passion for Evangelism
by Being Who God Made Us

At the end of a long week of training, I had boarded a crowded plane for a flight home. Exhausted and drained, I was looking forward to a much-needed nap. As I watched more and more people enter the plane, I realized that every seat was being filled. Finally the door of the plane closed, and I was grateful that the only seat left open was the one next to me. I thanked God for the chance to relax with a little space around me during that flight.

Then the door opened again, and one more person was allowed to enter. An elderly Chinese man stood in the front of the aisle, surveyed the crowd, and caught a glimpse of the empty seat next to me. He broke into a huge smile and worked his way back to my row.

It's OK, I told myself. *I don't have to talk to him. I can just lean up against the window and sleep.* I grudgingly told God that if he really wanted me to converse with the man, he would have to make it extremely obvious.

The man settled into his seat, looked over at me with a smile, and in very broken English, said, "Hello. You tell me God."

"Excuse me? . . . You want me to tell you about God?" I said.

"Yes. You tell me God."

OK, I asked for obvious, and that was obvious. I wasn't very happy about it, and I silently shared my grumpiness with God while asking him for strength and the right words. The next hour was centered on us trying to catch the meaning of each other's words and me talking loudly enough for the man's eighty-five-year-old ears to hear clearly (even more uncomfortable in a crowded plane). I was way out of my comfort zone and never would have initiated that conversation on my own, but it was one of those times that God had asked me to do something specific, and I had to trust him to work through me.

It was a good conversation. My seatmate was just learning English and found that talking with people was a great way to practice. Finally we both sat quietly. I felt like God was prompting me to give the man the "Four Spiritual Laws" booklet in my wallet, but I was afraid of starting up the conversation again. Just as we were landing, I prayed: *If you want me to give him the booklet, just have him bring up one more thing about God.* Within about ten seconds, he turned to me and said, "Thank you for telling me God."

I handed him the booklet, suggesting that it would be another way for him to practice his English and reinforce the things we had talked about. I also wrote down the name of a good church in his area where he could find more people to practice with.

Normally, that kind of conversation would have been a nightmare for me, but it was obvious that it was a divine appointment. I hadn't pursued it and had tried my best to avoid it, but it was freeing to know that I simply had to be prepared and responsive to what God wanted me to do.

Divine Encounters

Todd told me about a sign he passes each day in Scottsdale, Arizona, that welcomes people to their town. The motto says, "Most livable city." Twelve inches away is the block wall of a local cemetery, just a few feet from the cemetery driveway. The stark contrast puts the gospel in a nutshell. People drive down that busy street every day, living their lives, oblivious to the fact that someday they'll be turning into that cemetery driveway. No exceptions—eventually they'll all make that turn.

That's why we share our faith. It's not out of obligation or guilt or to fulfill some requirement of our religion. It's because God loves people and is deeply interested in what will happen to them when they turn into that cemetery. The reason the gospel is called the Good News is that it provides hope for what happens after death. As Christians, we're no better than anybody else; we've just discovered that Good News and have experienced God's love and forgiveness. He has given us the privilege of helping others experience it too.

We don't have to convince people of the truth of the gospel; that's God's job. Our job is to genuinely love the people in our lives and share the experiences of life with them. One of those life experiences is our faith, so it should be a natural part of our relationships to share that with them as well. Because of the eternal nature of faith choices, it's important to make sure we don't avoid communication about that part of our lives. The more we love people, the more we'll want to share our faith.

Even the term *share our faith* describes the process. We're not trying to force something on people that they don't want; we're *sharing* something that has changed our lives. If I go to a restaurant and order a dessert that turns out to be amazing,

I offer a bite to everyone at the table. I don't force it on them, but when they see my reaction, they generally want a taste. They don't grab my plate and take it from me, and they usually don't call the waiter over so they can exchange their dessert for what I ordered, but they had a taste, and they'll remember it. If it was positive, they'll think about it for a while, and they might decide to order it themselves on a future visit.

That's a great metaphor for evangelism. The Great Commission applies to all of us, no matter what our personality type, which means we need to be intentional about our efforts. Being shy or timid or uncertain isn't an excuse for not sharing our faith. Rather, it's the motivation to find out how God made us and become the best "me" we can be. Then we can focus on the natural process of sharing with others (our responsibility) instead of focusing on the results (God's responsibility).

You can impress people from a distance, but you impact them in one-on-one relationships. The emphasis in Scripture is to "be prepared to give an answer" (1 Pet. 3:15). So as introverts, the focus of our evangelism should be two-fold: *preparation* and *relationships*.

Preparation

People who spend a lot of time in airplanes generally become immune to the safety announcements, because they've heard them so often. But recently I read through the safety instructions in the seat pocket and saw more detail than is usually given verbally. The instructions said it's a good idea to keep your shoes on during the flight. If there's a need for an emergency evacuation, you'll be ready to go and not have to worry about stepping on broken glass or metal.

When we're told to "put on the whole armor of God" to face the battles of life, we're instructed to have our "feet fitted with the readiness that comes from the gospel of peace"

(Eph. 6:15). Though there are instructions in Scripture about taking action, this one specifically has to do with preparation. In effect, it says, "Put your shoes on." Then we'll be ready for anything we encounter.

If I intend to share Christ with the people he brings to me, it would make sense that I would prepare for those times. That means I've thought through a simple, logical way of presenting the gospel. I've found that thinking through my responses ahead of time makes the prospect of answering people's questions a lot less threatening.

There are many publications that outline the plan of salvation, but they need to become "ours." A good place to start is to read through different presentations, such as the "Roman Road," "Evangelism Explosion," or the "Four Spiritual Laws," gleaning the basic points that are common to all of them. Then take time with a close Christian friend to talk through the points, developing a customized version that fits your personality.

Several years ago, the company I work for wanted to make sure every employee knew exactly where the company was headed and what was important to the company. During a two-month period, we memorized the company's mission statement and values and were required to repeat them to our managers. There were prizes for timely completion of the assignment. One part of that process was to develop an "elevator speech" where we could answer the question, "So what do you guys do?" in one minute.

That process was one of the most valuable experiences I've had at that company, because it forced me to answer the question clearly and concisely. At least once a week, someone asks, "What do you do?" When they ask, I'm ready with a succinct response.

That should be even more true about our faith. If it means that much to us, shouldn't we be able to articulate it simply and concisely? Developing an "elevator speech" about our faith is a great way to handle those situations where a conversation turns to issues of faith. We've thought through our response and can present it clearly and naturally in the time it would take to ride an elevator from the bottom floor of a building to the top.

I also keep a copy of a simple tract, such as the "Four Spiritual Laws" or Billy Graham's "Peace with God," in my wallet. It's a way of being prepared for those situations where it seems appropriate to reinforce a conversation. It also helps when I want to share a particular verse but can't remember where it is. The booklet gives me the reminder I need.

Relationships

Relationships are like fingerprints: no two are alike. Every relationship I have is based on something that initially drew me and another person together and forms the basis for our connection. That means I handle every relationship differently: different dynamics, different interests, different temperaments, different ways of communicating.

Some of us are built for quality relationships rather than quantity. We don't usually seek out a lot of casual relationships, but we invest in a few deeper ones. That means we'll often be able to build trust with people who dislike shallow relationships. It's impossible to stereotype an introvert, since that quiet side manifests itself in different ways in different people. Introverts need to discover the communication tools that are part of their personal wiring, develop them, and use them to interact with others.

So if you're shy or reserved, how can you get started on the path of sharing your faith as a natural part of your daily life? Here are the things I've learned on my journey:

1. *Be around non-Christians.* Find ways that fit your personality to become involved with people who believe differently about Jesus than you do. Don't feel like you

have to share the gospel with them initially. Just build friendships.

2. *Be part of a team effort.* No one is solely responsible for leading someone to Christ. God uses many people in the lives of unbelievers to guide them toward faith. Our part is important, but it's not the only part. That's why God asks us to be faithful, not successful. First Corinthians 3:10 says, "By the grace God has given me, I laid a foundation as an expert builder, and someone else is building on it."

3. *Be creative.* Focus on the objective of leading people to faith, not on specific methods you've been taught. Think outside the box, asking God for creative approaches to building trust in the lives of others. Often it might involve writing instead of talking.

4. *Be patient.* If you haven't been sharing your faith for long, it will take time to develop your own style. Give yourself grace in the process; God does.

5. *Be unique.* Nobody can do evangelism the way I do; that's why God made me different from everyone else. The freedom I've found in that fact is a powerful incentive to share from love instead of guilt.

6. *Be available.* Some of us aren't made to recruit; we're made to respond. I need to develop my relationship with God and prepare for encounters he brings into my path. Then I don't have to panic when the conversation turns to spiritual things; I can simply be fully present with the other person during that time, listen carefully, and share my ideas without feeling threatened.

7. *Be aware of who the real enemy is.* It's not people from another faith. Those people simply have different backgrounds and beliefs than you do. I need to see them through God's eyes.

8. *Be involved.* Joining a volunteer organization that fulfills your passion is a great way to reach out to others. That

common area of interest gives you natural topics for easy conversation.

9. *Be intentional.* I've found it's artificial to try to work a presentation of the gospel into every conversation. Instead, we talk about other issues of life, but I drop in just enough comments so people know where I'm coming from:

- "Last Sunday I ran into someone *at our church* who found where to get a great deal on patio furniture."

- "Next week? Yeah, we can get together for coffee. Tuesday night I'm in a *Bible discussion group*, and Wednesday we've got family coming over. Any other night would be OK."

- "Yeah, raising preschoolers can be tough. I found three or four books that really helped us. *One was the Bible.* Another was . . ."

10. *Be directional.* Introverts tend to be unusually inwardly focused. We wonder how other people perceive us. In evangelism, we need to shift the direction of focus off ourselves and onto God. Our role is to point people's focus toward him, not toward us. If they're focusing on being like us, they'll be "looking for love in all the wrong places." But if our lives help them turn their eyes toward the Savior, he will have the opportunity to impact their lives.

That last principle is a great approach to evangelism: get people's eyes on Christ instead of on us. That enables us to simply be facilitators to get people looking in the right direction, and then we step out of the way and let God do his work.

conclusion

Several years ago, we were visiting my wife's parents in Bakersfield. We decided to spend a day with them on a short trip to a neighboring town. We couldn't take pets where we were going, so Gretchen, our miniature schnauzer, had to stay behind. There was no pet door in the house, so we had to leave her in the backyard for the day. Before leaving, we carefully checked for holes in the fence, gaps in the gates, and other possible escape routes for a curious canine. We placed a large bowl of water in the shade and left for the day.

When we returned that evening, she was gone. We searched with flashlights, called her name, and eventually walked around the neighborhood looking for evidence. There was no sign of her anywhere. We checked the fences and the gates again and couldn't find any possible way she could have gotten out. The only logical conclusion was that someone had heard her in the yard, climbed over the fence, and taken her away. We tried to encourage our kids to keep them hopeful, but I was thinking through how I would tell them Gretchen was gone.

After about forty-five minutes, my wife was calling Gretchen's name from the front yard and thought she heard a whimper through the fence. It took a while, but eventually, she heard it again, coming from the backyard by the outdoor spa. We still saw no sign of Gretchen, but we began to focus on the above-ground spa, which was surrounded by redwood siding that covered the spa's plumbing and electrical parts. The siding was individual slats of redwood attached to a framework. We finally realized that somehow Gretchen had gotten inside the siding—she was trapped under the spa. Careful inspection finally revealed that one of the boards was loose, attached only by a nail at the top. Somehow Gretchen had managed to find that board, move it out of the way, and crawl inside. The board had dropped back into place as though it had never been touched. She couldn't move it from inside the spa.

I moved the board aside and shone my flashlight into the darkness. I could hear her, but she had crawled all the way around to the other side. I called her name and could hear movement. Finally she appeared around the far corner, and I could see the light reflecting from her eyes.

I figured our crisis was over. I called for her to come and assumed she would race out of her accidental prison. But nothing happened. I called and called but was amazed that she simply stood still. She knew my voice; why wouldn't she come?

Then I realized the problem. I could see her, but she couldn't see me. I was shining the light directly into her eyes, and she couldn't see which way to move. So I turned the flashlight around and shone it in my own face so she could see me. Immediately she rushed through that open slat and into my arms.

That's one way to picture evangelism. Too often we think we need to shine the gospel on people's shortcomings and sins so it will be obvious where the problem is. But that's not our job. Through our lives, our words, and our relationships, we should be shining the light so they get a clear, accurate view of Christ. That's where they'll find the exit from the pain in their life. Jesus said, "I, when I am lifted up from the earth, will draw all men to myself" (John 12:32). We simply need to lead people to the Savior, not drag them or force them.

It's an exciting journey—one you might not have taken for a while. The destination is the same, but introverts have a different map than extroverts. Get the right map, take the first step, and you'll find a joy in sharing your faith that you never thought was possible!

notes

Chapter 3: Innies and Outies

1. Marti Olsen Laney, *The Introvert Advantage* (New York: Workman Publishing, 2002), 5.

2. Isabel Briggs Myers, *Gifts Differing: Understanding Personality Type* (Palo Alto, CA: Consulting Psychologists Press, 1980).

3. David Keirsey and Marilyn Bates, *Please Understand Me: Character and Temperament Types* (Del Mar, CA: Prometheus Nemesis Book Company, 1984).

4. Laney, *Introvert Advantage*, 20.

5. Ibid., 20.

6. Jonathan Rauch, "Let It Be," *Atlantic Monthly*, May 2003.

7. Linda Kreger Silverman, "A Developmental Model for Counseling the Gifted," in *Counseling the Gifted and Talented*, ed. Linda Silverman (Denver: Love Publishing Company, 1993).

8. Lesley Sword, "The Gifted Introvert," 2002, www.giftedservices.com.au/adults. html.

Chapter 6: The Fear Factor

1. Hans Selye, *Stress without Distress* (New York: NAL Penguin, Inc., 1974).

2. Betty Coble Lawther, *Woman, Aware and Choosing* (Brea, CA: MinMar Press, 1975), 40.

Chapter 7: The Graceful Witness

1. Rick Warren, *The Purpose Driven Life* (Grand Rapids: Zondervan, 2002), 17.

Chapter 9: What Would Satan Do?

1. Charles M. Sheldon, *In His Steps* (Grand Rapids: Revell, 1993).

Chapter 10: Methods That Are Biblical

1. David G. Benner, *Sacred Companions* (Downers Grove, IL: InterVarsity Press, 2002), 27.
2. Richard Byrd, *Alone* (New York: G. P. Putnam's Sons, 1938), 104.
3. Rauch, "Let It Be."

Mike Bechtle has a unique blend of ministry and corporate experience: from eighteen years in churches and Christian universities to more than two thousand time- and life-management seminars taught to many of the Fortune 500 companies. His articles have appeared in publications such as *Discipleship Journal*, *Moody*, *Eternity*, and *Entrepreneur*. He has been speaking at churches and conventions since 1974. After receiving his master's degree from Talbot School of Theology, he received his doctorate in higher and adult education from Arizona State University. For information about speaking engagements and seminars, visit www.mikebechtle.com.